MW00953806

The Faith

A Human Reality, a Divine Mystery

Reflections on the Faith Experience
An Existential, Psychological,
and Theological Perspective

Louis A. Marini

Copyright © 2022 Louis A. Marini
All rights reserved
First Edition

PAGE PUBLISHING
Conneaut Lake, PA

First originally published by Page Publishing 2022

ISBN 978-1-6624-7255-8 (pbk)
ISBN 978-1-6624-7256-5 (digital)

Printed in the United States of America

To Ada, my wife, my best friend, and love of my life, whose faith in God, commitment to family, loyalty to friends, abounding kindness to others, and optimistic approach to life inspired these reflections.

Our life is like a sailboat gliding into the sunset of the beyond. This passage is illuminated by the light of faith as we travel through the tumultuous waves of life. This light shines brightly within us guiding us all to a place of eternal refreshment, well-being, and serenity.

—Louis A. Marini

Contents

Acknowledgment

With much gratitude and appreciation to Cristina Priamo, who was instrumental in editing these reflections.

A Word from the Author

As I glared out from the seminary window on an autumnal late afternoon during a scripture class back in 1973, I could only wonder *What am I doing here?* I was aspiring to help people find God in their lives, but I realized shortly thereafter that my aspiration (as noble as it was) to help people discover God in their lives would be reversed.

Instead, my relationships with people would be the impetus of leading me to God. Many questions sprung up in my mind at the time. Will I persevere in my endeavor to pursue the ordained ministry? Will God give me the strength and opportunity of bringing comfort and empathy to others? Will I be able to be committed to Christian ministry for the rest of my years forsaking marriage and raising my own family?

What an enormous challenge or what an insane idea! This challenge was to allow divine presence to be experienced and permeate daily in people's lives. What has boggled my mind ever since continues to be "Can faith in the Divine be compatible with faith in humanity?" I don't presume that divine inspiration is experienced by everyone. However, I always believed that divine comfort and human empathy are intertwined.

I would like to venture that divine presence, as reflected in the faith experience, is where self-transformation happens.

I realize that many have coined the phrase *faith therapy* as a modality to discover the presence of the divine in their lives through treatment by utilizing one's religious belief system, e.g., Christian or pastoral counseling. I do not wish to pursue that avenue, but instead propose that faith can stand on its own in contributing to self-transformation just as well as psychotherapy. Faith is a human reality inherent in every human being and a gateway into the mystery of divine presence.

Whether faith is a nonreligiously based entity of humanity or faith in the Divine, they are complementary. They are correlated in achieving the goal of becoming unconditionally, totally, and fully human. This life pursuit is open to all and offers a golden opportunity to create a safer, healthier, and harmonious world.

I always wondered since beginning my theological studies forty-nine years ago, and being a former Catholic priest if faith in humanity and faith in the Divine can collaborate in this effort. Can faith as experienced in the human drama work in concert with faith in the mystery of the Divine so as to enrich one's spiritual and emotional well-being? Today, I revisit that same question in an ever-changing, fragile and turbulent world.

As I find myself entering a new stage in my life having left the ordained ministry voluntarily in 1994 to marry and, now, as a retired counseling psychologist after a rewarding practice of twenty-four years, I am still wondering if this collaboration is possible, which brings me to why I have decided to author this book.

I want to contribute and give back to the people I served both as an ordained minister and psychotherapist as I leave the academic world of research, teaching, and many years of clinical practice.

Secondly, I hope to share some insight about experiencing faith in the Divine and to ease any angst, restlessness, and anxiety of living in a world fractured by COVID-19.

Finally, I wish to embark upon a soul-searching adventure to make sense of life during these uncertain and unpredictable days amid social unrest and a global pandemic.

I hope I can remain true to these tasks to demonstrate how faith—a truly human reality—can provide healing within the perspective of the Divine.

Introduction

There is no *bona fide* definition of faith since faith is a multidimensional reality. The dynamic of faith is paradoxical for it can be inspirational by touching one's soul to conversion not always observed in action yet many times, this conversion is observed in action. Faith has to do with the journey, not the destination. The destination of faith as human reality is unity and harmony of life. The destination of divine faith is eternal life.

One consistent symbol of the faith experience seen as human reality and as divine mystery is the symbol of light. The *light* of faith inspires conversion of heart and consequently results in good behavior. This is not magical but the result of hard work that one invests in self-transformation. The en*light*enment born of faith supplies the energy and the resolve resulting in self-transformation providing for a richer spiritual and emotional life. A key factor of self-transformation is embracing and appreciating human relationships. Human relationship is the foundational building block for faith. Ultimately faith seeks unity of humanity and the unity of the human with the Divine through relationship acting as its binding force.

Another prominent symbol reflective of faith both as human reality and divine mystery is the symbol of the circle. Faith sees the circle of life to be infinite. The circle can be a vivid representation of the relationship of the Divine with humanity. The circle traditionally represents God as an infinite being having no beginning and no end. The theme of the circle of life prominent to faith was universalized in Disney's presentation of the *Lion King* reechoing how relationships are born, grow, change, die, and resurrect.

The purpose of these reflections is to understand how faith can grow from a tiny mustard seed of an idea to an enormous tree of infinite possibilities for every person. This endeavor can be accomplished without any bias since they are composed from a perspective of not only a Christian believer of the Catholic tradition but also one who believes in the power of psychotherapy.

This book consists of six chapters; while they are all interconnected by the theme of this book, each chapter stands on its own. For this reason, I recommend that each chapter be read separately.

Chapter 1: What do we understand by the phrase "I believe"? How does this colloquial expression become so familiar in our everyday language, and how does this expression relate to faith?

Chapter 2: It is a brief survey of the modern history of the crisis of faith, especially in our country. It examines "the fallout" caused by the Coronavirus pandemic in terms of our efforts to live faith despite all the ramifications.

Chapter 3: It explores how the language of faith is embedded in symbols. It demonstrates how a symbol brings to life both nonreligious based faith and faith that is enshrined by religious tradition.

Chapter 4: How faith as human reality can transition into the faith of the Divine. It explores the infinite possibilities of human relationship with God.

Chapter 5: It demonstrates how the Divine is mirrored in human experiences and validates what it means to be fully, unconditionally, and totally human.

Chapter 6: It offers a segue into how we can assimilate the effects of the twofold reality of faith as human reality and divine mystery into our daily lives.

I realize when all of us start a new book, we tend to skip over the preface or introduction and begin reading Chapter 1. In this case, the introduction sets the framework of how this work intends to tackle a fascinating and complex subject such as faith. So too, reading the epilogue is equally rewarding in understanding how all these complexities about faith are funneled together to make sense.

I wish to conclude with the closing selection of Dante Alighieri's *Paradiso of the Divine Comedy.* Just as with reflecting upon the experience of faith in the Divine, so too in *the Paradiso,* the light and the circle are prominent symbols of divine presence.

In the final canto (XXXIII), St. Bernard praises Mary, mother of God addressing her, "Humbler and more exalted than any other creature." Bernard then asks Mary to give Dante the power "to rise higher to his salvation." Mary moves "her gaze to the eternal light." Dante is filled with longing, to the limit of his desire, and his sight is now "becoming pure" as it rises to the light, his sight far exceeds his power of speech. Dante the poet addresses God in order to ask that he be given the power to describe it in writing his poem even in its most minor form. The light is so powerful that it overwhelms Dante's memory and ability to express the wonder of what he sees. Accompanied by his beloved Beatrice, Dante gazes into the light, which has "reached the Goodness that is infinite." He describes the "light" of God as like "three circles" of three colors, reflecting one another as rainbows and fire where he feels consumed utterly by the love that moves the sun and the stars.

In these closing verses, Dante describes the unapproachable and unfathomable light where he experiences infinite illumination reaching the Zenith of Life itself and is filled with the bliss and serenity of the eternal radiance of love:

Dante's Experience of Divine

O Light Eterne, sole in thyself that dwellst
Sole knowest thyself and known unto thyself
And knowing, lovest and smilest on thyself!
That circulation, which being thus conceived
Appeared in thee as a reflected light,
When somewhat contemplated by mine eyes,
Within itself, of its own very colour
Seemed to me painted with our effigy
Wherefore my sight was all absorbed therein,
As a geometrician, who endeavors
To square the circle, and discovers not,
By taking thought, the principle he wants
Even such was I at the new apparition
I wished to see how the image to the circle

Conformed itself, and how it there finds place
But my own wings were not enough for this
Had it not been that then my mind there smote
A flash of lightning, wherein came its wish
Here vigour failed the lofty fantasy;
But now was turning my desire and will,
Even as a wheel that equally is moved,
The Love which moves the sun and the others stars.
(Translation courtesy of The Literature Network)

Chapter 1

Believing: A Leap into Faith

> At the end of our journeying, we arrive at the
> place where we first started knowing it for the
> first time.
>
> —T. S. Eliot

Believing, what does it mean? What does it resonate in you? For some, it means hoping for a pleasant future event to happen. For others, it is associated with religious beliefs or social causes. For parents, it may be the high expectations they have slated for the future of their children. For others, it means expecting future success in business, career, and professional undertakings. For lovers, it means hoping that their relationship will have longevity. For those who are ill, it is the hope for a cure of their illness. For all of us for the past couple of years, it is the hope that the Coronavirus pandemic will come to an end.

Being a baseball fan, I remember growing up with the battle cry, "You gotta believe." It became the slogan of every New York Mets player and fan in 1969. The expression was coined by Tug McGraw, a relief pitcher for the Mets that year to inspire winning. It so happened that this mantra "You gotta believe" resulted in a world championship for the Mets.

Believing is not magical; it involves hard work. It can have miraculous results, even in real life. Believing is real, not virtual.

Believing can also take on the expectation that a child's fantasy can come true. This was clearly portrayed in the 2004 animated adventure film *The Polar Express*. The film tells the story of a young boy who on Christmas Eve sees a mysterious train bound for the North Pole stop outside his window. The boy is invited aboard by the train conductor played by Tom Hanks. The boy struggles with the childhood fantasy of believing in Santa Claus. He comes to the realization that to believe goes beyond being convinced that Santa Claus truly exists but that believing is a profound human reality that makes life worth living.

If we look up the meaning to believe in the dictionary, it says, "To lend credence to or hold to be true." Believing is an *intimate, existential, dynamic, relational, and visceral* human act.

Believing gives rise to beliefs. Beliefs are secondary in importance to the act of believing. Believing is living with a lifeline associating us with others. Beliefs are intellectual safeguards and convictions of the human act of believing. Believing unlike beliefs is infinite in scope not confined or conditioned by history.

In this chapter, I wish to focus on how believing is a "road map" and natural human disposition to faith and how faith is essential for what it means to be human.

Believing is a living natural inner drive that attracts one to the *Other*. The *Other* is defined as another human being. We believe together. For the most part, believing is a communal human activity. It gives us a sense of community, family, and belonging. On the other hand, a community of believers cannot substitute for individual believing.

W. H. Auden once remarked, "The relation of faith between subject and object is unique in every case. Hundreds may believe, but each has to believe by oneself."[1]

Nobody can do our believing for us.

Some people will believe in anything because their conviction costs them nothing. You can come up with a random list of beliefs for these people, and they will be content not because of their inner conviction or drive to reach out to the Other, but because they are accustomed to defending their lifestyles against the complexities and adversaries of life, so they believe. These people don't wear believing "on their sleeves." It is rather a disguise for those who don't care what they believe in or whom they believe in as long as they feel solidarity with popular demand.

However, when the individual is immersed in believing as a visceral act, it becomes an attraction to the Other. This attraction challenges the believer to be creative, sensitive, and committed to the process of self-transformation. This transformation offers the believer infinite possibilities to become a gift giver to another human being. Becoming a gift giver to another not only results in personal satisfaction but also contributes to the good of the Other and at the same time allows for self-discovery of one's own strengths and limitations.

Believing demands that one is committed unconditionally to the relentless drive of getting to know and being at service to the *Other.* I would define being at service to another as love. This process tests one's vulnerability of trusting that this knowing and loving will be reciprocated by the Other. Believing always means "believing in" a human being not merely adherence to concepts, ideologies, or systems. "Believing in" always necessitates relationship.

We tend to use the terms of believing and beliefs interchangeably, but I suggest that we distinguish them in our usage. When we speak of beliefs, it has to do with giving intellectual assent to doctrines, philosophies, and political or religious systems as compared to "believing in," which has to do with living the truth about oneself and exhibiting respect for the dignity and good of others. "Believing in" means entrusting yourself to another person—building your life with the help of others. It involves total and unconditional trust that replaces all human insecurity.

The hope of "believing in" will allow us to experience all the goodness, energy, inspiration, and joy that emanates from another human being that we enjoy as relationship.

The distinction between "believing in" and beliefs can be seen in this way. As an American citizen, I hold to the belief of life, liberty, and the pursuit of happiness for all. As noble as this belief may be, it becomes of no consequence unless it is grounded by *believing in* people. "Believing in" people means that this belief needs to translate into human behavior. It is not enough to hold this belief sacred as enshrined by the US Constitution. Believing expects that I need to exhibit respect in my behavior toward all human lives no matter the race, culture, ancestry, creed, age, gender, sexual orientation, or socioeconomic status. Beliefs are sacred only because they receive their meaning from the process of "believing in."

Believing demands that one be committed and invested in a life process of self-reformation. This means that one needs to take stock of one's behavior and make the necessary changes to augment one's strengths to be "other directed" while at the same time maintaining integrity of one self. It means living in a "we" world as compared to the "I" world we presently live in. This necessitates that one be humble enough to identify and own up to one's limitations. Self-reformation is the work of self-transparency admitting our shortcomings and need to reach out to others.

Believing needs the discipline of self-reformation and the inner strength of courage to accept the truth about oneself in adjusting to the complexities of living. When this process of self-reformation is repeated consistently, it results in self-transformation and sets the ground for faith.

Believing seeks its voice in faith. Faith is a virtue. A virtue by definition is a behavior showing high moral standards or a quality considered good and desirable in a person. Faith is not a fashion statement nor a crusade, but a chosen morally good lifestyle. Where believing has to do with what we are now, faith is the lifestyle of what we will be in the future, but it comes at a cost emotionally.

"I must be willing to give up what I am in order to become what I will be."[2] There is a risk in the act of "believing in," but it is a crucial first step if we are to walk in faith and not solely by sight. The risk in believing involves humility of self, "which is not thinking less of self but thinking of oneself less" so that one is not distracted in making life choices.[3]

C. S. Lewis once remarked, "Only a real risk has the reality of belief, for we are what we believe we are."[4] Believing is not a social expectation but a prerequisite for faith. Faith is the heart and soul of the human act of believing. "Faith is the assurance of things hoped for, the conviction of things not visibly seen" (Hebrews 11:1).[5] Faith is derived from the Latin *fides* and the old French term *feid* meaning *a confidence or trust in a person, thing, or concept.*[6] Faith is a gift of life that must be nurtured and loved into maturity. Faith needs us to be active agents; that is, we need to cultivate, we need to reflect, and we need to love the life of our faith. This doesn't eliminate the fact that we will not have doubts, but it does treasure what we care about who and what we believe in.

In the context of religion, one can define faith as "belief in God or in the doctrines or teachings of religion.[7] In the general context, this life of faith is a journey of the soul that seeks on what is *special* in the human heart. It drives one to be virtuous and good. It energizes the character of human beings not to be obsessed with "selfies" but to be responsible self-givers. Faith is a gift not earned, deserved, or achieved. It is not intellectually driven but driven by love in self-giving.

Faith's ultimate goal is to love. Love is the power that transforms the lover into the one loved.[8] The things that we love tell us who we are.[9] Faith is not merely an attitude nor adherence to teachings but always involves a drive toward the good. Faith is a human drive sharper than any sword and able to discern thoughts of the heart. This virtue is not bought or sold but a gift that calls for one's choice for what is good.

This good may be defined in many ways. It can be seen as taking responsibility for one's well-being—physically, spiritually, and emotionally. It may be seen as reaching out to others in need. It may mean replacing egocentric attitudes and selfish behaviors with altruistic ones. It means living by convictions where truth, justice, and righteousness are found. No one *deserves* gifts; we are blessed with them. No one is entitled to favors; they are gratuitous. Gifts and favors reflect the generosity of the giver, not the worthiness of the receiver. This is what faith is about. "To one who has faith, no explanation is necessary; to one without faith, no explanation is possible."[10]

For the one not religiously inclined, faith is the human expression of the act of believing without evidence. By faith, we accept as real what we cannot prove or see. We not only accept but even risk our future endeavors on the conviction that the purpose of our lives lies beyond the present.

By faith, we are continually challenged not to succumb or be slaves to what so often is taken for granted to survive. Faith involves possessing in advance what is hoped for, a way of knowing and loving realities not visibly experienced. Faith's subjects are exclusively human beings in relationship or as we shall explore later humans in relationship with the Divine.

When a person promises me something, I have faith in the person's words, as if I have already embraced the promised gift or completed task. When a trustworthy person tells me something that I cannot readily verify, it is through an act of faith in the person that I obtain knowledge of what has been communicated to me. This life of faith makes special and even sacred every moment in time of one's life, every space of one's situation, every action of one's decision, and even every thought in one's psyche. For this reason, faith, although a human experience, has a sacred dimension going beyond the tangible and to what is not seen. Faith doesn't lower our life expectations nor holds our heads in the sands, nor is it fascinated by personal whim but challenges us to excel as human beings.

Faith is grounded in common sense not wishful thinking. Faith is always accountable to truth and needs to be tested constantly in terms of what life presents. It is not kismet since we always have a choice to have faith. It is not viewing life through rose-colored glasses but accepting consequences from deliberate choices. "Faith is always seeking human understanding to flourish."[11] Faith has to do with discovering the truth about oneself with fortitude and honesty. Faith has to do with questioning ourselves about who we are and who we are in relationship with the world.

Faith seekers have difficult work to accomplish since making choices in living life is not all or nothing. "If you would be a real seeker after truth, it is necessary that at least once in your life, you doubt, as far as possible, all things."[12] Doubt doesn't compromise or destroy faith but tests and challenges our preconceived thoughts so that we can be stronger believers. If we become stronger in believing, we will in turn become effective gift givers to others. The gift we give ourselves is not "stuff" or favors that we exchange at holiday celebration, but rather sharing our time and talents with others. Time may be the most precious commodity we possess because we cannot get time back like reclaiming wealth or possessions. Once time is spent, it is gone forever.

The importance and value of our time is highlighted in one of the scenes of the movie *Gone with the Wind* where there is a sun dial outside of one of the establishments which reads "Do not squander time, it is the stuff life is made of." During the pandemic, some of us had more time than we knew what to do with, for others not enough time in the day to take care of their families. If there is a lesson learned during the pandemic, it is that time is precious. If we need to do for ourselves or for others to reconcile, reconnect, network, comfort, or just have fun together, we need not postpone it. Life is too short, and time is of the essence. We can share our talents, energies, and resolve to be at service to others. This is what self-giving involves. This is the work of self-transformation.

Faith as a human experience differs vastly from other human experiences. It differs greatly from politics because faith seeks truth whether convenient or inconvenient, never invested in individual agendas. Faith differs from various life philosophies since faith seeks truth in the concrete living of a relationship, not just wisdom to live by.

Faith transcends religion because it embodies in action the values or beliefs that religion safeguards. Faith in the religious context is a companion to theology since a good relationship with a human being has the potential to be grounded in a human relationship with the Divine. Faith has to do with believing that life is worth the work in living. Faith is only real when shared in love and in truth. Faith demands we become gift givers to others even when not convenient or self-serving. Faith becomes internalized in our behavior only when the believer is persistent and consistent in taking ownership of the demands of faith on a daily basis.

Faith drives us to discover the truth about ourselves even in the uneventful daily routines of our lives. Faith validates T. S. Eliot's description of life experiences, "Upon the end of our journeying, we arrive at the place where we first started knowing it for the first time." Our arrival at familiar situations in life realizing them for the first time is the insight that faith provides. Faith inspires us to bring new insight to the familiar beckoning us to act differently than how we acted formerly to bring about goodness.

To bring this discussion about believing and faith into the real and not to just engage in what may seem like spiritual double talk; I like to demonstrate how the human faith experience works.

Some thirteen years ago while in private clinical practice, I treated "Ana" who was desperately seeking solace and relief from insomnia triggered by her recurring night terrors brought on by obsessive, shameful, fearful, self-loathing thoughts.

Ana had suffered from panic episodes and melancholia for years but was reluctant to approach a mental health professional fearful of being judged as "crazy." She worked many years as a cook for a local restaurant despite being afflicted by persistent depression. However, the precipitating cause of Ana coming to treatment was the incarceration of her adult son who was convicted of a violent crime and sentenced to twenty-five years to life in maximum security.

When I worked with her to process her grief during our eighteen sessions to ameliorate her depression, I was intrigued to ask her what made her so driven to continue to visit her son on a weekly basis, traveling almost three hours each way using public transportation. Her response was simply and emphatically: "My son deserves to be in prison for what he did, but I visit him because he is my son."

After the course of treatment of helping her confront and resolve her intolerable inner rages of anger, loneliness, humiliation, shame, and guilt, it dawned on me that she was not driven to visit her son sheerly out of religiosity or guilt. She impressed me by her "believing in" her son despite his crime. It was her steadfast faith that made her a persistent and persevering gift giver. She believed that reaching out to her son would in some way not necessarily make him more contrite of what he had done but manifest her deep faith in him. She wanted him to experience by her loyalty that she still valued him as her son despite his crime.

I do not know what ever became of Ana, but I do know that she achieved insight about herself in therapy both acknowledging and experiencing a power arising from faith to act as a loving mother and healing instrument.

This is exactly where "believing in" becomes the catalyst for a lifestyle of faith. This behavior goes beyond the desire to believe in something but in *someone*. This story beckons us to rewrite the old adage of "To sin is human, and to forgive is divine" to be rewritten as to be truly, fully, and unconditionally human is to be divine.

To be divine is to be intensely present to the *Other* without condition, judgment, or retribution. The act of believing transforms one by allowing for an unbelievable, relational, existential, dynamic, unconditional, intimate, and visceral human response to address a dire human need.

Another recollection in my life travels where believing results in the human faith experience comes to mind. In my first pastoral assignment as a young priest in the late 1970s working in an Italian and growing Latino community, my faith in the Divine was both challenged and validated through the unexpected and spontaneous generosity of that community.

I had been providing religious instruction for Lucia, a twenty-year-old woman who wished to receive her confirmation. Lucia was the daughter of Italian immigrants living with them along with her elderly maternal grandmother and younger brother. Weeks into the instruction, I had learned that her family suffered a devastating house fire causing them to be temporarily displaced after just moving into the parish from Brooklyn.

I attempted feverishly to approach the ecclesiastical authorities to obtain financial relief for the family without much success. My only alternative was with the family's permission, to spearhead with a few parishioners to solicit from the neighborhood funds, food for the family, and needed refurbishments for their house. The outpouring of love and generosity from the people of the parish was so heart-felt that it echoed throughout the entire neighborhood. This family of five remarked that it was the best Christmas present they have ever received considering that they had struggled economically in

Italy prior to migrating to the US. The generosity of the community unquestionably went beyond their religiosity. Many of the people who contributed admittedly were not practicing Catholics but were so moved by the dire human need of this family that they became gift givers. This is what it means to be "believing in" the *Other* and where faith is born. This is a case where religion takes a back seat to faith. The beliefs we accept in religious faith need to be inculcated in the living of faith as self-givers. Faith demands that we become gift to others to make life meaningful.

Human beings such as Ana's and Lucia's family cannot live without hope. Hope is at the forefront of faith. Hope exists for them because they acted lovingly. Hope varies from person to person, but it the essence of the faith experience. It can induce ambition and heroic action. Hope can stir desires, plans, and aspirations. Hope can also make people fearful of the future or even selfish at times. However, what hope will do is to drive one to believe in people and in turn move others to faith. Whenever we hope in people, we strengthen them and lessen their anxieties. If we sense that someone in need has hope in us—not just in what we can do for them—this makes us gift givers. This engenders trust and credibility in our relationships.

The patient endurance of the giver of hope is a vocation of the believer. Hope risks everything. It is high stakes for the believer. When we hope in human beings, we are bonded to what happens to them and always run the risk of being taken for granted and vulnerable by doing this, but hope is key to believing. It makes the act of believing dynamic and existential. Those in dire need were moved viscerally by those who generously responded by being totally present to them. They believed in the goodness of people who responded selflessly. Those in return who generously responded believed in the goodness of those in dire need viewing them as precious human lives. Those who generously gave of themselves not only felt good about it but also felt special in being life changers. Life givers are life changers.

Believing is a bilateral dynamic experience. Faith fuels that hope whether blessed or cursed with the ability to face the fears of the future and to respond courageously through action. Essentially, human beings cannot actualize themselves without the power of faith in someone so that life can be good, meaningful, and worthwhile.

The value of human life is not predicated by one's intelligence, importance, or status as much as it is by one's altruistic choices to respond as a gift giver to others. Faith involves personal choice to be gift givers. It involves believing that being present totally to others and in turn acting lovingly can be the difference between life and death. Faith needs to be relational and grounded in community for no one is an island nor does anyone alone have all the answers to life's questions.

Another example of how believing is existential of the human spirit can be seen in the legendary novel *Of Mice and Men* by John Steinbeck. In the novel, the character Crooks, a black disabled farmhand alienated on the farm because of the color of his skin, is trying to convince Lennie, a mentally challenged farmhand, that everyone needs to trust in at least one person in their life no matter how much or what one knows. Crooks tries to reassure Lennie and quell his fears that his farmhand partner and best friend George will return soon after his trip into town. Crooks who read his employer's books daily to pass the time since he was unable to do physical work goes on to say to Lennie, "Books ain't no good. A guy needs someone to talk to him because life gets too lonely; it can make a guy sick." This is where faith cries out for human relationship that is the fertile ground that makes believing possible. Relationships needs to be the medium of human empowerment that we call faith. Humanity cries out for relationship with other humans. Faith needs human relationships. Human relationships need faith.

It is important to discern what faith is and what it is not. "There are two ways to be fooled. One is to believe what isn't true; the other is to refuse to believe what is true."[13] A major contributor of studies in the human faith experience belongs to one of the most influential theologians and philosophers of the twentieth century—Paul Tillich, a prolific German author and Lutheran minister who escaped the Nazi regime and came to the US where he became a dynamic teacher and charismatic preacher. Tillich was a German American Christian, existential philosopher, and Lutheran Protestant theologian.

Tillich is best known for his works *The Courage to Be* (1952) and *Dynamics of Faith* (1957). In academic theological circles, he is best known for his major three-volume work *Systematic Theology* (1951–1963) in which he developed his "method of correlation," an approach that explores the symbols of Christian revelation as answers to the problems of human existence.

The major focus of his work was to take the existentialism, a philosophical inquiry that explores the problem of human existence and centers on the lived experience of thinking, feeling, acting individuals and apply it to Christianity. Each individual, not society or religion, is solely responsible for giving meaning to life and living it passionately, sincerely, and "authentically."[14] All meaning and truth derive from how humans process the world. Truth arises from the responsibility one takes for one's choices. Existentialism emphasizes that the existence of the self depends upon seeking truth as what it means for the self as opposed to the long traditional approach of scholasticism that emphasized that truth can be discovered by understanding the essence or nature of things. Tillich applied the existential approach to understanding that the ground of being or existence can only be understood in terms of understanding that the Divine (God) is the ground of being.

Tillich is considered the father of the Christian existentialism. He considered existentialism as an element in a larger whole, as an element in the vision of the structure of being in its created goodness, and then as a description of the meaning of human existence within that framework. For Tillich, human existence cannot be explained or understood by any other philosophy or way of thinking but to understand that God (the Divine) is that ground of all being. What makes faith what it is, is precisely that *faith is above all the state of being ultimately concerned.*[15] The dynamics of faith are at the very heart of one's existence.

Humanity has many concerns: cognitive, aesthetic, social, and political. Some of these concerns are urgent, often extremely urgent, and each of them can claim ultimacy for a human life or the life of a social group. "If the concern claims ultimacy, it demands the total surrender of one who accepts this claim, and it promises total fulfillment even if all other claims have to be subjected to it or rejected in its name."[16] Tillich gives an example of seeing faith as one's ultimate concern. If a national group makes the life and development of the nation, i.e., nationalism, its ultimate concern, it demands that all other concerns such as economic well-being, health care, family life, education, aesthetic and cognitive truth, justice, and humanity be sacrificed. The ultimate concern, in this case nationalism, becomes the center of existence for its citizens. Nationalism is "likened to a god" for this national group. Nationalism becomes the citizens' ultimate concern.

I recall working a clinical case early in my practice where a couple came to treatment over intimacy issues. The presenting problem was that one of the partners in the relationship devoted her entire time and energy to the care of her elderly father who was a widower. This care was at the expense of time with her partner. This resulted in relationship estrangement where the drive to know and love the other (her partner) diminished over five years to the point they experienced each other as strangers not lovers. In this case, the patient made her father the object of ultimate concern of her life, and this was a blow not only to her relationship with her partner but also to all her friendships and eventually to her career leaving her unemployed. Although this is a negative example, nevertheless, this is the meaning of ultimate concern. Faith demands this total surrender of the one who accepts this claim; all other human concerns are to be sacrificed.

Secondly, *genuine faith is a centered act and act of the total human personality.*[17] Tillich sees faith as the most centered act of the human mind. Faith is not the sum total of all positive human personality traits but transcends each and every one of the traits and transcends the total of all of them. It is not enough to have the plenitude of good individual traits such as honesty, truthfulness, integrity, generosity, sincerity, mercy, forgiveness, compassion, courage, empathy, kindness, affection, patience fortitude, etc. Faith transcends each and the totality of all these good personality traits. Faith transcends all rational or nonrational (emotional) elements of humanity in an ecstatic passion for the ultimate.[18]

Thirdly, *humanity is driven toward faith by one's awareness of the infinite to which one belongs, but which one does not own like a possession*.[19] The source of faith is a "restlessness of the heart" within the flux of relative and transitory experiences of ordinary life. St. Augustine of Hippo in his *Confessions* clearly voices these sentiments in discussing his need for conversion by seeking the infinite and divine, "Late have I loved Thee, O Beauty so ancient and so new, late have I loved Thee! Thou didst call and cry out and burst in upon my deafness; Thou didst shine forth and glow and drive away my blindness; Thou didst send forth Thy fragrance, and I drew in my breath, and now I pant for Thee; I have tasted, and now I hunger and thirst; Thou didst touch me, and I was inflamed with desire for Thy peace… Thou hast made us for thyself, O Lord, and our heart is restless until it finds its rest in Thee."[20]

Faith is that infinite passion or insatiable appetite for the infinite. Faith comes from hearing not necessarily an audible voice but "a voice in the heart." This goes beyond the subjective meaning of faith as a centered act of human personality to what is meant by an act of living itself. Tillich expounded that the object of faith can be construed as God but faith remains to be the unconditional and ultimate concern.

According to Tillich, atheists are not excluded from the conversation of unconditional and ultimate concern which faith is. "Everyone has an ultimate concern, and this concern can be an act of faith even if the act of faith includes the denial of God as it does for the atheist."[21]

Fourthly, *faith brings us in touch with the holy*. Holiness is not understood in a moral perfection sense of the Protestant ethic or described in the ritualistic devotions and piety of Catholicism but in the original sense as found in the Hebrew scriptures of being separated from the world and of finite relations. This is the reason why religious groups have always worshiped in separated places. These places of worship are separated from the mundane. Since there is no finite way to approach the infinite, faith needs the power and medium of holiness to transcend beyond the world to the infinite, the ultimate of existence. Holiness has to do with righteousness, which is the drive for truth and justice. Holiness is that justice and truth for humanity where one can approach the infinite reality. When holiness becomes this morally good and logically true reality, it becomes a creative force and no longer divorced completely from the world but acts in concert with world as a creative force called grace. Two hallmarks of holiness are awesome mystery drawing fascination and "shaking" terrifying presence. These components of holiness were introduced by Rudolf Otto's work in expressing humanity's encounter with the holy (In Otto's terminology: *mysterium fascinans et tremendum*).[22] This means holiness is an awesome creative mystery and at the same time an attractive, fascinating, and yet unapproachable, awful reality.

Tillich describes the relationship of human faith and holiness:

The human heart seeks the infinite because that is where the finite wants to rest. In the infinite it sees its own fulfillment. This is the reason for the ecstatic attraction and fascination of everything in which ultimacy is manifest. On the other hand, if ultimacy is manifest and exercises its fascinating attraction, one realizes at the same time the infinite distance of the finite from the infinite, consequently, the negative judgment over any finite attempts to reach the infinite. The feeling of being consumed in the presence of the divine is a profound expression of man's (humanity) relation to the holy. It is implied in every genuine act of faith, in every state of ultimate concern.[23]

Faith provides a perspective on humanity's frustration to deal with the infinite distance between the finite (humanity) and the infinite (Divine) by providing an enduring hope that the infinite can influence humanity. In other words, it is possible for humanity to have a relationship with a reality that is unattainable—the Divine.

Another aspect of faith that makes it unique is that we cannot discuss faith unless we allow for human doubt. Faith is an awareness of an element of certainty and an element of uncertainty. To accept this condition requires courage. Faith is not empirical as the sciences are. Faith demands that I make choices based upon selecting the good "behind the blind curtain" of life. What if there is nothing "behind the curtain" of life? This is the reality of human doubt. It is in the midst of uncertainty that faith shows its dynamic character. If all is certain and empirical, there is no cause for faith.

While I was in clinical practice working in a hospital, I had an interesting conversation with my colleague who was a psychiatrist. Besides being a terrific professional and humanitarian, he was at best an agnostic not really convinced in an afterlife. Our conversation centered upon this very point on whether believing in a divinity or afterlife was worth the while. I remember telling him as a believer, if there is nothing after death, I will never know it. However, if there is eternal life, then I am in luck. He chuckled and responded that my answer demonstrates good logic, and he was impressed with the fifty-fifty odds, but he remarked, "Logical or not, you still need to believe." With these odds, what the risk of faith is about, in short, is human doubt.

If faith is understood as belief that something is true, doubt is incompatible with the act of faith. The risk of faith is human doubt. The doubt that accompanies every act of faith is the doubt of one who is ultimately concerned about a concrete expectation in one's life. This doubt differs from methodological doubt that is found in scientific research in establishing a hypothesis or from skeptical doubt that is basically an attitude toward all beliefs. The doubt we are discussing may be identified as an existential doubt. It does not question whether a special proposition is true or false as in scientific research. It does not reject a concrete truth about a certain belief system whether religious, philosophical, or political. But it is a human doubt implied in faith that accepts this insecurity and takes into itself in an act of courage. I need to be courageous to doubt. I need to be courageous to believe because of the ultimate risk of failure.

Faith includes this courage. Any act in which courage accepts risk belongs to the dynamics of faith. Doubt is not a permanent experience within the act of faith but always lurking and present when I accept faith. Doubt is not a negation of faith but keeps the believer honest. For Tillich, existential doubt and the act of faith are poles of the same reality, that reality being one's ultimate concern. Serious doubt is a confirmation of faith not a denial of faith. Doubt indicates the seriousness of one's ultimate concern, its unconditional character. Human doubt makes the believer stronger in one's convictions. Doubt is not denial of faith but keeps faith accountable.

Finally, the last component of *human faith is that it exists exclusively in the life of the community. Faith does not exist in a vacuum.* Faith is not an individualistic endeavor or goal but one that always involves interaction with others. Whether it be another human being or group of people, faith always involves a relationship. Like every act in emotional and spiritual life, faith needs human language and community to grow. Without language, there is no religious experience or expression, and hence there is no human act of faith. Religious language enables the act of faith to have a concrete content. A good example of this is in the Judeo-Christian tradition, the scriptures are the language of the symbols, myths, beliefs, and historical sacred events authored by the community of believers to both understand and have a relationship with the Divine. Creedal formulations, liturgies, and even the recorded historical sacred events need language of a culture for the act of faith to have expression and be alive and relevant. Tillich will argue on the importance of the community as the place where the act of faith exists in describing Christianity:

From the Christian point of view, one would say that the Church with all its doctrines and institutions and authorities stand under the prophetic judgment and not above it. Criticism and doubt show that the community of faith stands "under the Cross," if the Cross is understood as the divine judgment over man's [human] religious life and even over Christianity, though it has accepted the sign of the Cross [as center of the act of faith]."[24]

Faith is not an exercise of intellectual pursuits. It is the pursuit of life.

Knowledge alone is not the source of faith. Knowledge is needed for faith to seek understanding, develop, and be expressed in language for a culture, e.g., theology. This means that faith transcends the language of doctrine and creed and goes beyond the world of beliefs that are conditioned by time and history. One doesn't need knowledge to attain faith, but knowledge validates the one who has faith.

Neither is the source of faith based on an act of the will. It is not that I will believe but rather I have the courage to believe. Human volition is instrumental in the sense I may have the noblest intentions and desire to will that I can commit to a conviction. However, mere willful choice to believe doesn't ensure faith. Faith is not an intention but a life I am committed to with my entire being. If I am not convinced of faith existentially merely willing, it is futile. I can will to be a good citizen, but if I do not behave by complying with the expectations and demands of being a good citizen, it is futile. The same is true of faith. I cannot will myself to believe. I need courage to believe.

Neither is the source of faith based on emotions or feelings. Faith claims truth from its ultimate concern and its commitment to it not because it "makes me feel good" or "feel better about myself." The power of faith alone doesn't make me a good person. That is magical thinking. Faith is the conviction that can awaken positive feelings that enhance but do not cause faith. What makes me a righteous person is allowing faith to embrace my entire being that in turn can make me feel good, joyful, and self-fulfilled by doing good. As a believer, I can experience joy, hope, and love with a way of living that guides my life. I have embraced that lifestyle of faith but the feelings that may accompany it didn't cause my faith but are the fruits of faith. The power of faith needs to be embraced and translate into good behavior. Emotions alone do not bring faith into action behaviors do.

If this were the case, all people who are sad, in pain, or even depressed would not live in faith. This is as inaccurate as if I were to say conversely that people who are always happy, optimistic in life, and joyful live in faith. I need to make the act of faith my ultimate concern and priority in my behavior as a human being.

Let's test this faith experience with the following exercise by following the assumption of the premise: *Humanity is basically good; the choices one makes determines good or evil behavior.*

To avoid any bias, I will devoid from any religious or spiritual connotation or any connotation from the behavioral sciences, psychiatry, or other medical disciplines to interpret this premise. Simply taken, human beings from birth to death are basically good. Take this statement on faith. There is no empirical data globally to prove or disprove it since that would be impossible to ascertain. This statement is not an indisputable fact. This statement is based solely upon personal experience validated by the experience of others from observing life. There is no empirical, nor scientific proof or law of nature to attest to this statement's validity. It is a statement made in faith about the goodness of human nature based upon what people ordinarily demonstrate or observe about others.

Another approach is defining that human faith experiences can be viewed by referring to a model of the development of faith across the life span. This faith development theory is attributed to James H. Fowler, PhD. His stages relate closely to the works of Piaget, Erickson, and Kohlberg who are noted experts in psychological development in children and adults.

For Fowler, faith is considered as a holistic orientation regarding the individual's relatedness to the universal. Fowler identifies seven developmental stages of faith:[25]

Stage 0. *Primal period.* An infant lives in a foundational state of either trust or mistrust depending upon the care the infant receives and its sense of safety in the world. It is from this foundation that preliminary image of "God" begins to form that will affect future religious perceptions (from birth to two years of age).

Stage 1. *Intuitive-reflective faith. This is the stage* when the child is first able to use speech and symbols in organizing thoughts and experiences. It is also the period that many children begin their religious education. This is a period where children without the logical processes that allow for discernment or questioning simply assume that what they are taught by their care givers is the only possible perspective. Religion is learned mainly through experiences, stories, images, and the people that one comes in contact, e.g., parents tell the child God lives in heaven (three to seven years of age). So, the child begins to believe that God exists.

Stage 2. *Mythical-literal.* The information provided to the child is accepted readily without question to conform with social norms ("elementary school": ages seven to twelve). The child attempts to make meaning of what was previously fantasy.

Stage 3. *Synthetic-conventional* faith. Children question their own thoughts as part of creating identity and building relationships with the world outside the immediate family. Any conflicts with one's beliefs are ignored at this stage due to the fear of threat from inconsistencies (early-late adolescence: twelve to adult).

Stage 4. *Individualistic-reflective faith.* The individual critically analyzes adopted and accepted faith with existing systems of faith. Either disillusion or strengthening of faith happens in this stage. The person steps out of the circle of interpersonal relationships that have sustained his or her life to that point. As one can reflect on one's own beliefs, there is an openness to a new complexity of faith, but this also increases the awareness of conflicts in one's own belief. The goal of this stage is understanding. The individual takes personal responsibility for his or her beliefs and feelings ("early adulthood": mid-twenties and over).

Stage 5. *Conjunctive faith* (mid-life crisis). Individual realizes the limits of logic and facing the paradoxes contradictions, divisions, or transcendence of life accept the "mystery of life" and often returns to the sacred stories and symbols of the preacquired or readoptive faith system. This stage is called negotiating settling in life (mid-life: thirty-five and over).

Stage 6. *Universalizing faith.* This is the "enlightenment" stage "where the individual comes out of all existing systems of faith and lives with the universal principles of compassion and love in service to others for upliftment without worries and doubt."[26] (It is a universal faith rather than an individual one functioning in a transcendent reality rather than a material one detected in middle to "late adulthood": forty-five years old and over.)

According to Fowler, individuals pursuing faith need not complete all six stages. There is a high probability that most individuals to be fixed in a particular stage for a lifetime, i.e., stages 2–5. Stage 6 is considered the summit of faith development and often considered as "not fully" attainable.[27] This model of Fowler demonstrates that faith is intimately associated with the development of what it means to be human and can be viewed as a basic ingredient of human development not something extrinsic to it.

In summary, faith may utilize knowledge, activate the act of the will, and move the emotions but always transcends beyond each of these faculties and is more than the total of them. Faith is a rhythm of life. It is existential and holistic of all human potentials and systems. Faith makes life worth living with an inner drive toward the infinite, in pursuit of the good, grows with what is holy, accepts doubt as part of believing, and always thrives in community. The greatest gift of human life is to know and to love and to be known and to be loved. This is the promise of faith.

The human experience of faith is "believing in" someone beyond oneself for the purpose of self-revelation and extending loving service to the *Other*. The journey of faith is a very fluid life process that seeks the truth about self and how this is negotiated with one's relationship with the world. Faith is an intangible reality unable to be measured either qualitatively or quantitatively. Faith is the realization and conviction of what is hoped for—evidence of realities unseen that give life purpose and meaning. Faith is an interior transformation, a firm assurance, a strength of holding things together with a calm fearlessness.

Faith in action exhibits the integrating power of healing within the self and self with others. The integrative power of faith is distinguished from what others refer to as "faith healing," which is the attempt to heal others or oneself by mental concentration on these powers in others or in oneself. Rather, what the integrative power of faith is happens in a concrete situation where there is a relationship between subject and object (the other) where something happens not magically but a change of heart or transformation caused by the mere encounter or "presence" of two human beings. An openness for each to accept the other mutually results. Analogously, this happens in psychotherapy too; however, the only difference is that faith deals solely with one's ultimate concern where in psychotherapy the therapeutic relationship between therapist and client to stir change in the client may not be related to the client's ultimate concern.

Faith in action results in love. However, the question remains: is there love without faith? Faith as defined as a set of defended doctrines or beliefs doesn't produce acts of love. However, faith as the state of being ultimately concerned implies love since if love is present; even if not evident, it is embraced by faith, which drives the longing and desire for union with one's ultimate concern.

Faith without knowledge is blind. Faith with knowledge is wisdom.

Faith without wisdom is myth. Faith with wisdom is enlightenment.

Faith without hope is an allusion. Faith with hope is confidant reassurance

Faith without love is absent. Faith with love is eternal.

Chapter 1 Summary

- Believing is a human, intimate, existential, relational, dynamic, and visceral act.
- Believing is an act of "believing in" human beings.
- Beliefs, doctrines, and ideologies are secondary and are in service to the act of "believing in" a person.
- "Believing in" is the first step to faith always necessitating a relationship.
- "Believing in" is a persistent, lifetime process of knowing and being present to the Other.
- The Other is identified as another human being or in the realm of religion the Divine.
- "Believing in" risks vulnerability since knowing and loving the Other expects no reciprocity.
- Believing seeks its voice in faith.
- Self-transformation is the fruit of "believing in" another human being.
- Self-reformation is the work of transformation to correct one's shortcomings and increase one's accountability as a responsible human being.
- Self-transformation is the result of taking responsibility in actualizing one's strengths and owning up to one's limitations.
- Becoming a self-gift to another is the goal of self-transformation.
- Faith is a human drive that is a gift—not earned, purchased, or obtained.
- Faith is the heart and soul of the human act of believing.

- Faith is believing without the evidence, grounded in reality and common sense open to vulnerability and doubt.
- Faith is real and not virtual grounded in truth, steadfast in hope, and manifested in love.
- Faith:
    - is one's ultimate concern in life.
    - is a centered act of the entire human personality not just positive human traits.
    - is a passionate drive and attraction toward the infinite.
    - is an experience of the holy that separates one from the mundane.
    - is always understood and appreciated within the sphere of human doubt.
    - only lives within a believing community.
- Faith **is not**
    - solely a matter of the intellect, i.e., not I know, therefore I believe.
    - solely a matter of the human will, i.e., not I desire, therefore I believe.
    - solely based upon human emotion, i.e., not I feel, therefore I believe.
- Stages of faith in terms of human development:
    - *Primal (prestage):* Infant total dependence for well-being and safety on parents—beginnings of development of "image of God" from foundational state of trust fostered from the care the infant receives that shapes future religious perceptions.
    - *Intuitive-projective:* A child is first able to use speech and symbols in organizing thoughts/experiences where religion is learned mainly through experience, stories, and images via parents or with others the child comes in contact.
    - *Mythical-literal:* A child docilely accepts information without question to conform to social norms.
    - *Synthetic-conventional:* Children question their own thoughts as part of creating identity and building

relationships with the world outside their immediate family.

- *Individualized-reflective*: An individual critically analyzes the adopted and accepted faith of the family of origin and challenges it against other existing systems of faith.
- *Conjunctive faith:* An individual realizes the limits of logic facing the paradoxes, contradictions, or transcendence of life and returns to sacred stories and symbols of preacquired or readoptive faith system. Individual attempts to negotiate these symbols with life situations.
- *Universalizing faith*: An individual comes out of all existing systems of faith and attempts to reach the universal principles of compassion, love, and service.

Chapter 2

Crisis of Faith

> It was the best of times, it was the worst of times, it was the age of wisdom, it was the age of foolishness, it was the epoch of belief, it was the epoch of incredulity, it was the season of Light, it was the season of Darkness, it was the spring of hope, it was the winter of despair, we had everything before us, we had nothing before us, we were all to going direct to Heaven, we were all going direct the other way—in short, the period was so far like the present period, that some of its noisiest authorities insisted on its being received, for good or for evil, in the superlative degree of comparison only.
>
> —Charles Dickens (*A Tale of Two Cities*, 1859)

The year 2020–2021 was the best of times and the worst of times in our country. The best of times witnessed the depths of unselfish love human beings exhibited toward their fellow human beings even to the point of risking their own lives. These unshakable heroes were physicians, nurses, and health care professionals risking their lives to have done the unbelievable in treating COVID-19 patients. Dedicated teachers instructed our young despite the overwhelming challenges of both virtual or in-person learning. Hardworking food suppliers risked their safety to ensure that Americans would have food on their table. Steadfast transportation personnel ensured safety for travelers who needed to get to work daily. Courageous law enforcement, resilient firefighters, untiring paramedics, and other emergency frontline professionals shielded the community from harm. Restaurant proprietors feeding the hungry despite their own financial hardships endured due to the lockdown as mandated by state government. Humanity showed its good face.

On the contrary, with the relentless spread of the coronavirus in all its variant forms accompanied by misinformation disseminated on all levels, the course of defense against the virus, the subsequent unplanned, inequitable and at times chaotic distribution of the vaccine was the ugly side. This along with the polarization of the public on these issues was enabled by the political blame game as played by our two political parties in Congress by relentlessly disputing measures affecting public health that stalemated financial and medical relief to the masses. This was the unforgiveable and ugly side. The deaths of over eight hundred thousand Americans and counting due to the pandemic featured the worst of times in our nation.

Despite all the social, health, and political upheaval, we lived amid a crisis of faith in our nation. We lived through the shadows of uncertainty and helplessness searching for truth, serenity, and relief. We found very little solace in the devastating months of 2020. The little we found was due to the unselfish resolve of medical professionals despite the apparent indifference exhibited by many of our political leaders. We struggled to find the light of faith in the midst of the darkness of the night of terror. When did this faith crisis begin? What caused this crisis? Who is responsible? Does it really matter?

The answers to these four questions respectively are as follows: this crisis has occurred repeatedly in history. It always seems to occur when there is a lack of public trust in those who are entrusted to lead and protect our communities. We are all responsible. It is paramount to humanity that crises of faith be resolved.

Many today are experiencing a crisis of meaninglessness in their lives. Religion has traditionally supplied a framework for the individual's quest for meaning but the institution of many major traditional denominations seems to have failed in this regard (especially during the pandemic) to perform this function any longer.[28] Pews are empty in places of worship not solely due to social distancing but also because of a lack of confidence in religious leadership. Churchgoers have doubted their religious traditions and grown skeptical of their religious leaders and wondering if they are really in step with what was happening in our world overshadowed by the pandemic. Religion in the public forum had remained silent for the most part and voices of leadership of our spiritual leaders were muted and retreated into locked churches. Other than Pope Francis's historical and monumental visit to Iraq in March 2021 meeting with Ayatollah Ali al-Sistani, one of Shite Islam's most authoritative figures in demonstrating solidarity by voicing the conviction (in the pontiff's words), "That fraternity is more durable than fratricide, that hope is more powerful than hatred, that peace more powerful than war,[29] there was very little to applaud religious leadership during the pandemic. Both political and religious leadership had failed miserably in providing a harbinger of hope, reassurance, and serenity that the nation could survive this pandemic spiritually, emotionally, and mentally.

In response to the initial four questions concerning the crisis of faith, let us begin with the first inquiry, when did the crisis of faith begin?

Attempting to understand the repeated cycle of crises of faith in history, we can begin by studying in modern times how faith was enormously challenged. Globally we begin by studying how the onslaught of the radical philosophy espoused by Friedrich Nietzsche of nineteenth-century Europe vastly influenced the Western world challenging traditional religious values. Nietzsche proclaimed that science was so evolving and feared that man's great strides in science without parallel advance in ethics and self-understanding would lead to nihilism.[30] Nietzsche pointed out that if a society loses its center of values it results in waves of massacres, chaos, barbarism, and tyranny as the middle twentieth century witnessed with the rise of totalitarian governments and the world at war. Nietzsche suggested that the traditional values of Judeo-Christian belief system was no longer relevant to humanity. He called for a transvaluation or revaluation of all values. Nietzsche went beyond the agnostic and atheistic thinkers' criticism of faith of the seventeenth and eighteenth centuries where rationalism prevailed over religion.

Nietzsche espoused a radical existential philosophy that deemed religious belief as irrelevant to humankind. He proclaimed that "God is dead." He professed that the values based upon what is good and evil as dictated by religion provided no meaning for humanity. The existence of a deity and the afterlife were viewed by him as an allusion. Nietzsche accused contemporary classical philosophies of lacking a critical sense and blindly accepting dogmatic premises in their consideration of morality.[31] Nietzsche accused philosophers of founding grand metaphysical systems upon the faith that the good man is opposite of the evil man, as compared to Nietzsche's philosophy that viewed the good man as a different expression of the same basic impulses in the evil man.[32] Nietzsche's system of thought that became rampant in nineteenth-century Europe replaced the classical philosophic traditions of "self-consciousness," "knowledge," "truth," and "free will" with the "will to power" as an explanation and goal of all human behavior. He endorsed a perspective of life that is "beyond good and evil" denying a universal morality.[33] Nietzsche perceived man as the master of his destiny whose potential for power is unlimited through the human will. This notion affirmed that human beings can achieve the highest intellect not held by the moral code of good and evil but goes beyond it to a sort of "superhuman" dimension.[34]

Another global movement challenging the world of faith was the Age of the Enlightenment of seventeenth and eighteenth century Europe disseminated intellectual, philosophical, scientific, and cultural changes as advocated by Isaac Newton, John Locke, David Hume, Jean-Jacques Rousseau, Voltaire, Montesquieu, Spinoza, and David Diderot who paved the way for the political revolutions of the eighteenth and nineteenth centuries including both the French Revolution and the Revolutionary War in America. Their philosophies and scientific theories questioned traditional authority and embraced the notion that humanity could be improved through rational change. Fixed dogmas of Church teachings and authority came under fire by advocating individual liberty and religious tolerance with its emphasis on rationalism, scientific method, and reductionism. This enlightened period of rationalism gave way to the wildness of romanticism in the nineteenth century, followed by liberalism and twentieth-century modernism. The Age of Enlightenment prepared for radical philosophies of Nietzsche and others attacking traditional religious values held sacred from the Renaissance period. These movements attempted to replace religious faith with sheer rationalism and reductionism to explain human existence.

Other such historical developments causing a crisis of faith for individuals and families came about in our own land too. This is clearly evident by the earth shaken effects of the many wars and military expeditions that our country had engaged since the two world wars up to the struggles resulting from the withdrawal of US troops in Afghanistan. With all these wars and bloodshed, no one really wins, but everyone loses. How could there not be a crisis of faith in the nation let alone in humanity?

Another national historical movement that challenged the faith of our country came about with the atheistic movement in the 1960s initiated by Madalyn Murray O'Hair who founded the American Atheist Center and the Society of Separationists. This movement began a national outcry to refute all faiths and endorsed a vast crusade to eliminate religion from the American culture. It propagated the belief that religion violates the US Constitution, which ensures the separation of church and state. All these attacks were attempts to dissipate one's belief in the Almighty by demonstrating the absurdity of religious faith. On a human faith level, this atheistic movement, similar to the age of reason, replaced the belief in the human spirit with sheer rationalism and pragmatism. This allows for all ethical decisions in life to be reduced to pragmatism. This basically means if a life decision is practical and works, it is morally good.

This denies that there are universal moral standards that hold human behavior to a higher standard. This tenet of atheism that denies the existence of any deity embraces that humanity is only accountable to itself. When you reflect upon this, atheism is very short sided. It not only negates the existence of the divine as far as religious faith but also reduces the meaning of human worth to mere utilitarianism on a nonreligious faith level. Utilitarianism is a doctrine that all human actions are justified solely if they are useful or are beneficial to the majority. What about actions that threaten the individual's freedom?

There are many human actions that are pragmatic and seemingly good but may not necessarily be morally good. There needs to be a universal moral standard to which human behavior is accountable. With this understanding, which is diametrically opposed to what atheism proposes, it calls for all human life to be cherished and protected. Atheism not only discredits belief in the deity but also discredits the potential inner drive of the human person to utilize faith as the ultimate concern to achieve infinite human possibilities.

Another seemingly setback to faith in our country occurred in March 1984 when the Senate defeated the prayer in public school amendment endorsed by President Ronald Regan. This did not sanction religion to be taught in schools but called for students in the classroom to have the option to take momentary time-outs privately and quietly to reflect in their respective faiths. Again, there has been precedents in the history of crises of faith both globally and nationally. Crises of faith are not novel but have always been around in history.

Our second inquiry: How does a crisis of faith happen? This usually occurs when there is a breakdown of public trust in those who are mandated to serve the public good, socially, politically, and religiously. Currently the legitimate institutions of our day whether it be the institution of government or religious institutions have been under public scrutiny due to the lack of leadership, initiative, transparency, and adequate outreach with their constituents or congregants during the pandemic. This is evidenced not only by extensive public criticism but also by the significant rise of mental illness in our society due to anxiety and at times hysteria over the unknown effects of the spread of the virus.

The failure of the institutions of Church and State to proactively reassure the public that they can survive these turbulent times is greatly disappointing. This could have been avoided by launching more proactive means to educate and initiate immediate social services, financial, medical, and pastoral resources to reassure the public that they are in safe hands to create a sanctuary of relief to combat COVID-19, where federal, state, and city governments have been tardy and disorganized in coordinating efforts to respond to the spread of the virus, as we have repeatedly seen a significant lack of trust and cynicism grew challenging the credibility and transparency of government. A crisis of faith and skepticism in government's ability to lead generated doubt about the government's transparency to communicate the truth about the course of the disease and cogent plans for the future termination of the pandemic cost the lives of over eight hundred thousand Americans and rising. Mixed messages given by politicians to appease the public for self-serving agendas aggravated the dilemma. Not only was government at fault but also the voice of leadership and the limited initiatives of outreach of many Christian churches and other traditional religious institutions remained relatively passive and mute during the pandemic. This is a crisis of faith. Whether it be political corruption, "cover-ups," misplaced priorities, slow responses of government to deliver economic relief to the public, or scandalous clergy sexual abuse, all these contribute to public skepticism. This contributes to a communal crisis of faith.

Addressing our third inquiry of who is responsible for a crisis of faith, we need to look at ourselves and own up to one of the troublesome current trends in our nation today. Here the culprits are among us. This is evident when people not only dissent with established institutions or the medical community but also go a step further by their own intransigence by "pitching up their own tent" to solve social or health issues disregarding the law or taking the law in their own hands despite negative consequences. This happens when people propagate self-serving agendas motivated by their own personal biases or political persuasions. This is not only a danger to our democratic system of government but also disruptive of faith in the human family. This is where diversity that needs to result in unity unfortunately replaces unity. This occurs when people become so intolerant of each other's values and unwilling to listen before taking mindless action based upon sheer emotion. The result is anarchy, chaos, and violent demonstrations of hatred that are never acceptable for those who walk in faith. To rid us of this rise of arrogance does not devalue the individual rights of freedom to voice one's personal opinion, but encourages dialogue to communicate with diverse opinions. That is what they are—mere opinions not facts or doctrines. Opinions are only opinions everyone has one.

History repeatedly teaches us that this misdirected approach of intolerance and injustice are the story of national revolutions in government and heresies in religious movements. This mentality where people are so intrenched in their own opinions and voice their position as unquestionable doctrine without listening or having intelligent dialogue is an erosion of society. This intolerance is destructive of the human spirit and counterproductive of faith. This mindset results in behavior that demonstrates bad faith or no faith at all in the community and negates the freedom of the human spirit. What we are left with is not the freedom of speech ensured by the Constitution, but what I call "reckless license of speech" where people promote hateful interactions toward others and label those whom they disagree with as inferior, unpatriotic, and irreligious. The result of this is a complete polarization in society and a breakdown of human communication.

The current climate of constant politicizing every issue under the sun, which many times we accuse politicians, has become today's norm. This leads only to discord, hatred, and bigotry. These days you cannot discuss politics, religion, or even sports intelligently without vehement reaction in families or among colleagues and fellow Americans. Human communication has broken down and has become contentious. Contention becomes contagious and incorrigible.

Faith cannot exist let alone thrive in this toxic environment.

The scientific origins of the coronavirus are still being investigated by the international medical community to probe the origins of COVID-19. For the present, it can be attributed to the workings of nature. Although this may seem to be too simplistic an answer, what is not simplistic is how we have dealt with it. We didn't create the virus or "start the fire," which has been burning since the world's been turning, as Billy Joel sings in his famous 1989 hit, but we can keep the fire going by our arrogance, irresponsible behaviors, and apathetic attitudes.

Our indifference and lack of empathy toward those who tirelessly do the right thing to respect the health of others keep the fire burning and the virus thriving. This is another troublesome trend in our nation at present that is very disturbing and doesn't seem to subside nor inspire faith.

The mentality that as an individual and as an American, "this is my right" (no matter what the issue) with no awareness of the common good not only is selfish but also demonstrates that one's decision is misinformed and irresponsible. Many have overreacted emotionally with their decision-making faculty becoming a defective "compass" in making good judgment. Unfortunately, this took the symbol of the face covering as a controversial issue as with whether one wishes to be vaccinated or not as some felt was a violation of exercising one's individual right.

Both scenarios were highly politized causing polarization in our country that turned ugly. Aside from all the medical protocols that were recommended to remain safe, we are all responsible in contributing to either containing the spread of this pandemic by our vigilance and adherence to medical protocol or its spread by our own arrogance and entitlement to think that we are beyond it. As we experienced the horrors of COVID-19, it didn't allow us to retreat into our own comfort zones of indifference, greed, entitlement, and apathy easily and selfishly. This would negate everything expounded in the previous chapter about the dynamics of believing.

Hopefully, by the time this book is published, the Coronavirus will be history, and our fight against it will be over; however, it is the continuance of this arrogant spirit that will not allow us to return to some semblance of normalcy as a people. It is over simplistic to put the entire blame on our institutions or to place our unrealistic expectations on the medical community. We need to take ownership from what we learned from the pandemic to take care of each other. We need to utilize the power of faith as gift givers to combat not only the pandemic but also negativism that has grown rampantly in our land.

It does nothing but make us helpless. The virus, even when defeated, remains a symbol of all that is wrong with humanity.

The pandemic brought us to our knees. The pandemic as we painfully discovered caused a tsunami of grief for millions who witnessed the global deaths of so many lives. It is on our knees that we need to pray, be humble, and reflect on where our lives stand today and how much we embrace the value of human life and need to take care of each other. The care of each other commences with the realization that not only is my life preoccupied about my rights as an American but also my behavior needs to be mindful of the consequences of the common good that many times was overlooked during the world before and certainly during the pandemic.

Humility, sometimes called the queen of all virtues, is the lens we need to see life through to recognize that the common good is a complementary part of our human rights. Faith presumes that individual rights are commensurate with the common good. Faith with hope urges us to hold in esteem human life. This will be the only way we are to become true citizens of this planet and return to some semblance of normalcy.

Each of us can find ways great or small to be stewards of that mission. The arrogance of indifference toward others as witnessed during the spread of the pandemic is descriptive by a line from the lyrics of Billy Joel's song from "Only the Good Die Young": "I'd rather laugh with the sinners than cry with the saints—the sinners are much more fun." Applied to the horrific health crisis we experienced, this can be applied in so far as it is much more pleasurable to retreat into our cocoons of security at the costs of those who struggle with the bitter consequences of the disease instead of reaching out to them. Being at service to others in time of need is more difficult and less fun than being content living in our sedentary lives of indifference, selfishness, and comfort.

Our response to our final inquiry of whether faith is essential to the future of humanity is a resounding yes! Humanity depends upon the goodwill of us all by exemplifying attitudes of hope and utilizing responsible and healthy behaviors. We need to stomp out negativism in all its forms. Just as being advocates of issues such as global warming, the responsible use of the world's natural resources or ensuring solid education for our children or the protection of all stages of human life or safeguarding occupational opportunities for all, and treating all people with respect of their human rights, our choices today have consequences for future life of the planet.

All human lives matter is the rally cry of faith. We are all responsible for the well-being of our communities but need responsible leadership from government and our faith communities "to walk the talk" of healing and reconciliation. We all need to walk the talk of faith. Allowing disease, racial injustice, or threats to human life run rampant because of fear, ignorance, hatred, and entitlement will have catastrophic results. This doesn't enhance faith in humanity but enables despair. Alfred Hitchcock was once quoted as saying, "Despair is the immorality of the modern world."[35] The propagation of despair and devaluing human life in our world today is viewed in what the late Pope John Paul II called "the culture of death."[36] Faith is not the culture of the dead but of the living.

It is not my intention to engage in a political commentary or polemic, but it is my intention to give some context and perspective where faith is applicable during all this confusion and human suffering. In my opinion, there are four major current cultural trends that endanger faith. These trends are blatant, unforgiving, and cancerous of unity.

The first concern is the apparent danger flowing from social media in propagating conspiracy theories that not only transmits erroneous information but causes confusion, consternation, and hostility in human communication. Frequently and unfortunately falsehoods and manufactured facts (fake news) arise in social media at light speed so that the one who receives them is defenseless to either refute, clarify, or dismiss expeditiously as compared to what one would do in an in-person discussion. It is much easier and safer to dispute with another and verbalize what is on our minds in "light speed" utilizing social media rather than in-person since one doesn't have to deal with the fallout, confrontation, or retribution as with in-person interactions.

Social media, which in many ways began innocently as an efficient means of communication and keeping in touch with friends and family, can also be a curse at the same time. This occurs when its use is dismissive of others without allowing the one who receives the message an equal voice to have recourse to respond adequately. Frequently, social media has been utilized in being counterproductive in forging relationships of any kind when it produces information that is based upon shoddy reporting or based solely upon hearsay. This fosters animosity and bad faith. All these factors mitigate faith and don't enhance it. My expectation—and I'm sure the expectation of most who use social media—is that in all its forms, it needs to have integrity of truthfulness and respectfulness of others. All of us not only need to be sensitive and take responsible measures for the content of our communication but also do the due diligence in using reliable sources and presenting it correctly with an attitude of openness and respect.

When I think of communication, I can't help but recall the voice of the long-time public address announcer Bob Sheppard nicknamed "The Voice of God" by Reggie Jackson, for his smooth distinctive baritone and precise, consistent elocution that became iconic at both the old Yankee Stadium and Giant Stadium. Bob Sheppard was once asked, "What is the best way to communicate?" His response was "In communicating, one needs to be *clear, concise,* and *correct.*" I think we can all learn from these words of wisdom whether we engage in personal encounters or in social media.

A companion to communication is the long-forgotten human quality of personalism. Personalism as found in person-to-person communication always outweighs social media and remains the optimum means on all counts because it is real human presence. This presence cannot be replicated, replaced, manufactured, or virtually represented with the same potency by any other medium let alone by social media. The person "in the flesh" is the best medium of social interaction. Human presence is powerful and transforming especially when we talk about faith. Just like the expression "a picture is worth a thousand words," so too human presence speaks more than a thousand Tweets. Similar to when we have the unpleasant experience of attending a funeral of a deceased of loved ones, we express our condolence in words and in gesture, but our presence speaks volumes. Our presence says, "You are so important to me that I desire to be here with you to share your grief." Texting the message or sending a sympathy card or a flower arrangement no matter how thoughtful doesn't quite have the same potency.

Secondly, another concern in our present-day culture that hinders faith is the propensity of many people to have the compulsion to utilize social media to communicate every thought, every feeling, and every opinion on every issue at all times. This also includes transmitting every activity that they experience daily as if only their lives matter, and others are missing out in life or communicated to "correct" others to the extent that it is dismissive of others. This arrogance accentuates the narcissism of the sender of the communication and so attests to their judgmental attitude of seeing oneself as sole arbiter of what is "politically correct" or not.

This doesn't foster faith but nourishes bad faith. I never quite understood what politically correct means. I looked it up in the dictionary and found "exhibiting or failing to exhibit political correctness." Exactly what does this mean? Who exactly decides what is politically correct or not?

This expression is at least linguistically ambiguous. It has become a catch phrase in social media used to be dismissive at best of contrary opinions. As with political correctness, the compulsion to voice one's opinions in vehement reaction via social media is not freedom of speech but rather to call it for what it truly is—a compulsion. This is to use the old expression *neurotic behavior*. When neurotic behavior is aligned with judgmental unrealistic expectations of what others should think and do or else, it results in antagonistic behaviors typical of many of our human interactions these days. It doesn't promote positive human communication nor cultivate relationships but fuels vitriol.

This dysfunctional interaction may lead to an experience of "hollowness" of self and an estrangement of the self to others. It has the potential to cause one to lose perspective of self in relationship to the world and stirs a cauldron of resentment and agitation for the individual who harbors these poignant feelings. This pattern of behavior eventually results in the polarization of relationships in families, among friends or colleagues. The fun pleasantries of what would be leisure conversations turns sour on any issue where social interactions turn into vehement intransigence. Faith cannot flourish in this social toxic environment.

Thirdly, another inclination alien to faith in today's social media culture is frequently rash judgments made based upon one's subjective perception determined solely upon the optics of a situation or of a person's behavior as made from afar. The problem here is that mere perception may not be reality. If launched into social media, this perception may have potentially disastrous social or even legal consequences. This is not only a disservice to others and risks damaging reputations but also so alien to what faith is. This results in possible distortions of reality and how conspiracy theories are born. Conspiracy theories thrive on false perceptions constructed by one's bias.

This is not the world of faith. Faith is real and always in pursuit of truth. Just because I believe something to be true doesn't make it true. This thinking is not only delusional but also potentially dangerous for it promotes falsehoods and potential unfounded scandals.

On a humorous note, I recall in episode of *Seinfeld* where George Constanza, one of the prominent characters as played by Jason Alexander, responds to his best friend's (Jerry Seinfeld's) advice about the importance of being honest with yourself in dealing with relationships. George responds to Jerry by saying, "I will not be influenced by others' opinions of me anymore. If I believe it, it's true." This mentality today is very common for many who put much credence on what they read on the internet.

In this regard, we need to adhere to a quote attributed to Edgar Allan Poe who said, "Believe only half of what you see."[37] What you see and read needs to be researched, checked out, and obtained from reliable sources not accepted blindly from social media regurgitation. Frequently these "supposed facts" as displayed on social media become constructs of conspiracy theories and other falsehoods that people enjoy passing on to others. This is the antithesis to faith. Faith seeks truth, not sensationalism. The casual practice of passing on unfounded data is based on a dire need to obtain acceptance from others and a sense of wanting to be relevant by "getting the scoop" on people and events before others do.

This is similar to those who write the headlines for newspapers do. Frequently, those who compose the headline for the newspapers are not the same person who write the article. Frequently, the headline is an exaggeration of the article to get readers' attention. This is similar to those who declare their own opinion based upon unfounded data as fact. It is the definition of "fake news," which is infectious and contagious behavior rampant in our social media culture. It is ironic, however, that those who vehemently cry out for the freedom of speech voicing their opinions as fact are equally intolerant of others who also have a right to voice their responses based upon their convictions. This irresponsible behavior is not only done in bad faith but also no faith at all.

The intolerance to exclusively voice one's own opinions drowning out others whether it be on political, religious, or social issues causes increased animosity and negates any healthy relationship or faith in any person. This rampant practice in our society usually results in assaultive interactions, slander, and hatred. This is an exercise of "reckless license of speech," not freedom of speech. All freedoms bring with them inherent responsibilities. Freedoms with no concern for consequences are not freedoms at all but "reckless license" to speak or to act.

In fact, that is the difference between the freedom of speech and the reckless license to speak—recognizing that speech as with many other human rights has consequences one needs to be accountable. All human rights recognize that justice is not only ensured for the ones who demand it by their speech but also to be rendered to those whom the speech is directed. Faith cannot sprout from a terrain where freedom of speech becomes "reckless license" of speech. This apparently seems to be the landscape and the tenor of communication or the lack thereof in our nation today.

Faith can only come about from a unity of purpose of a people honoring diversity and based upon truth not on convenient data.

Faith is based upon the integrity of truth and what is real and held sacred in our lives not necessarily to what is convenient or self-serving. Although faith is based upon the truth, nevertheless, it is grounded in reality and common sense with always the common good in mind. Life decisions made solely for the good of the individual without the common good in mind are rarely faith-based decisions.

Another area of concern that is counterproductive to faith is the tendency to arbitrarily discard or cancel out past historical representations by individuals or groups who deem these to be offensive, racial, or bias. This has become known as the "cancel culture." This mindset emphasizes either the rewriting of history or whitewashing past recorded events to acquiesce to current political or social thinking. Rewriting history in this light is a distortion of the science of recording the past that is what history is all about whether good, bad, or ugly. The cancel culture attempts to allow the ends to justify the means by its insistence that the ills of the past need to be changed by canceling out the legacy of the past. This is not only an affront to the art and science of historical recording but also shortsighted by becoming the ultimate moral monitor that of itself is also historically conditioned and can easily be canceled out by subsequent generations.

Who is the authority to determine this? Accepting historical events on their own merits whether good or bad doesn't necessarily condone the ills of society of the past but further highlights the need for constant reform. Faith on the other hand deals with the misgivings and ills of the past by challenging them and demanding ways to reform them in light of truth and justice so that they will not be repeated. Rewriting history based on today's politics and what many may deem "politically correct" negates what has really happened and demonstrates no appreciation of history good, bad, or indifferent.

This would be utterly mindless and comparable to rewriting our own past histories based on our changed positive current self-perceptions. This would be a distortion of what really happened in our lives even though we may not be proud of it. It is in being critical of past ills and choosing better alternatives that allow us to change for the better not by merely canceling out our past as if it never existed. The same holds true of historical figures, events, literature and films, historical artifacts, and the naming of edifices after historical personalities.

Removing statues of George Washington our first president and a founding father of our nation from public because he was known to be a slave owner doesn't do anybody any good. This demonstrates an ignorance of history and a lack of common sense since it doesn't do anything to raise the moral conscience of people that slavery is immoral. No matter how deplorable slavery is, current political and social thinking cannot be the ultimate moral monitor for erasing history.

It needs to be social action that comes into play not canceling legacy that promotes change. It is ironic however that many who advocate for cancel culture are the same people who cry out against censorship as a violation of their first amendment right of freedom of speech. Again, is this freedom of speech, or is this "reckless license of speech"? We too will be judged by future generations and run the risk of being canceled out because what we aspire to today may not be compatible with the political or social thinking of the day in the future. Cancel culture, as with being politically correct, are shallow constructs not based upon common sense but stand on shaky ground because of their sheer subjectivism and arbitrariness to stir drama in society in attempting to initiate social change.

Cancel culture doesn't inspire change; social activism does. This mentality is not faith based. Faith-based reform calls for hatred to be overcome by love, revenge and bigotry to give way to forgiveness, and discord to be transformed to mutual respect. Only this approach will be a game changer for humanity. Canceling a person is a modern form of ostracism in which a person is thrust out of social or professional circles arbitrarily and stigmatized in social media in the form of group shaming. It easily is a gateway to conforming to the politics of the day and conspiracy theories. In the words of former president Barack Obama who notably criticized "woke cancel culture" (though not using the words as such), "Easy social media judgments are not social activism and doesn't bring about change."[38]

What about faith in crisis then? How does this relate on a personal level? What seems to be an essential issue as we continue to proceed into the twenty-first century has been the reoccurrence of what haunted the middle decades of the twentieth century—the human experience of emptiness. By this, I mean not only that many people do not know what they want; they often do not have a clue of what they feel about what they want.

I discovered in the twenty-four years of clinical practice when patients described their own plights in life that motivated them to begin therapy, it soon became evident that the underlying problem was that they had no clue of their own desires or wants. They generally discussed what they *should* desire, but very few came to therapy to work on themselves to be more productive human beings and more loving people or deal with the existential issues of faith. It became very clear that many were living their parents' expectations and dreams or rather they were attempting to overcompensate for their own inadequacies but not feeling in touch with themselves, a sort of depersonalization.

The American dream became an obsession for many and unreachable for others leading to high anxiety, distress, and depression. This malaise of emptiness has overshadowed us into the twenty-first century and has been exasperated by the pandemic. However, it finds its beginnings in earlier times by many having unrealistic expectations of themselves and never being in touch with their emotions. This has since resulted into a population of depression where the world is viewed as hostile place resulting in a melancholia of life. This is attested by the fact that there has been a rise in the number of suicides among the young from the ages of sixteen through mid-twenties since the pandemic.

The irony that we were faced with is that this malaise of emptiness that clinically is diagnosed as depression intensified due to protective behaviors recommended by the CDC to protect us and others from COVID-19. These safeguards included social distancing, wearing face coverings, constant testing, the vigilance of acquiring the vaccine, and basically avoiding contact with people as much as possible. These behaviors that are all valid to stop the spread of COVID-

19 paradoxically defy what humans inherently are—social beings. This resulted in high anxiety, a sense of hypervigilance, helplessness, hopelessness, feeling disconnected with the world, melancholia, and emptiness.

Again, the irony here is these safeguards intended to control the spread of COVID-19 and utilized to save lives became counterproductive to personal social interaction. This situation in turn increased the need for social media at the expense of person-to-person human contact. Social media has progressively replaced the personalism of person-to-person contact. We cannot blame the virus for all our emotional or spiritual ills but our choice whether to reach out to others and the manner we chose to reach out will determine our mental and spiritual well-being.

Rollo May, one of the originators of the humanistic psychology movement of the twentieth century, focused upon enriching the value of personalism and human interaction. He described those who become estranged from the world and not able to feel life as the "hollow people."[39] Many of us today can identify to some degree with Rollo May's clinical observation and recall the prophetic words of T. S. Eliot in defining this inner experience of emptiness:

> *We are the hollow men*
> *We are the stuffed men*
> *Leaning together*
> *Headpiece filled with straw. Alas!*
> *Shape without form, shade, without colour,*
> *Paralyzed force, gesture without motion…*
>
> *Our dried voices, when*
> *We whisper together*
> *Are quiet and meaningless*
> *As wind in dry grass*
> *Or rats' feet over broken glass*
> *In our dry cellar.*[40]

Hollowness in this respect doesn't connote being disingenuous or pretentious but rather experiencing lifelessness or having a bitter taste of life or no taste at all. It sounds much like describing one of the symptoms of COVID-19, doesn't it? Social media to a significant extent has replaced in-person interaction for justifiable reasons due to COVID-19 by allowing to maintain our lifelines with those who are important to us. Paradoxically, social media has sadly replaced personal presence with virtual representation. The quality of human interaction and living human presence has also unfortunately decreased. I hope moving forward personal human interaction doesn't become a thing of the past. I hope we can recover this important presence, which is an important ingredient in being human.

The sole reason why I retired from my clinical practice was exactly this decrease of human presence as found in personal interaction. It has always been my clinical philosophy that for therapy to be optimally efficacious, I need to engage with patients in-person to experience "presence" and reciprocate that same power of presence to the client. This makes the therapeutic relationship real not virtual. It makes one tuned in empathically not just sympathetically.

I experienced for many years that this real interaction caused dramatic changes to happen for my patients. Personal therapy of any sort and any modality, along with medication if needed, will help patients with their mental illness more than if they were merely on medication treatment alone. The reason for this is basically because personal therapy processes and renders the patient with skills and insight for change to deal with their issues where medication treatment treats the symptoms not the issues.

I did not find the use of a phone session or for that matter the use on Facetime, Skype, or Zoom with a family to my satisfaction. In fact, many of my patients shared that same feeling toward the last days of my practice when they told me it was unfortunate that we could not meet in person to discuss issues. It wasn't the same. The "magic" was gone. Clients told me therapy in person made them feel listened to, empowered, alive, and real. This failure to maintain personalism vis-a-vis person-to-person contact is a shortcoming not only for therapy but also for faith. Although social media has provided a benefit during the Coronavirus health crisis, it has at the same time been a source of social distraction.

Other than the experience of hollowness, another characteristic of our time is loneliness. This experience is described by many people who suffer from depression as being "on the outside," isolated, or feeling empty. Feelings of emptiness (hollowness) and loneliness go together. Loneliness gets confused with aloneness, which is of itself a positive behavior. Solitude allows us to reflect, think, gather, and reevaluate ourselves. Aloneness allows us to refuel and ensure that our feelings and thoughts are grounded in reality. We need to do this often. We need as human beings the opportunity to reflect and gather ourselves emotionally and spiritually especially before making crucial life decisions. This "self-time-out" is essential before interacting with others in relationships. We need to be alone more than we think.

There are many healthy behaviors we can engage in when alone: meditation, prayer, writing in a journal, singing in the shower, walking our dog, painting, working out, playing a brain buster game, solving a puzzle, baking a favorite recipe, reading a magazine or an enthralling novel, or just taking a quick nap. Aloneness can be a healthy escape to appreciate and develop a tolerance for private time so that we can unclutter our thoughts, sort out our feelings, and enjoy the solitude and silence of just "being" and doing nothing without needing an excuse.

However, feelings of loneliness do not provide much comfort. They usually occur when one experiences the discomfort and impatience, which results from not being familiar or how to be alone. Sometimes experiencing loneliness results in feeling stranded or uncared for and losing oneself in the process. Human beings get their original experiences of being a self out of one's relatedness to other persons weeks after birth. This quickly gets reversed as the infant transitions into becoming a toddler looking to be independent and self-sufficient without mother.

When one is alone without other people, one fears the loss of self. The experience of relating to another begins with the bonding of infant with the mother. From that point on, the reverse natural process is set into motion—the process of individuation of a human being. Here the human being seeks meaning as oneself relates to another and to the world. We call this self-autonomy. The fear of being alone derives much of its intensity from our state of anxiety lest we lose our awareness of ourselves. Thus, the expression fear of "losing one's mind" comes into play. As a result, the feeling of terror and panic of being lost totally becomes real and devastating. It can be compared to the feelings that a toddler experiences when lost and separated from the parent at the mall. It is the feeling of terror as if one was tied to the railroad tracks while an express locomotive is approaching. Terror is not just a nightmare but exists in real time. The same is true of one's faith. When a human being loses self where faith begins, there is the experience of nothingness and not feeling grounded. This is sheer terror.

Loneliness like emptiness and hollowness are all experiences of terror. Loss of self is a loss of our minds, our hearts, and in turn relationships. In its extreme form, this fear of losing one's orientation is the fear of psychosis. It was my experience as a mental health professional that when people are on the brink of psychosis, they often have an urgent need to seek human contact to ensure being grounded and not being lost. This need for human contact is what bridges them to reality. This is where social acceptance whether one is mentally challenged or estranged because of race, color, gender, creed, socioeconomic status, or sexual orientation discovers the power of self-awareness and tenaciously holds loneliness at bay.

Social acceptance in the form of "being liked" has the power to dissipate feelings of emptiness, loneliness, hollowness, rejection, and depression. A human being surrounded and absorbed comfortably by the warmth and compassion of another will develop inner resources of perseverance, strength, and a sense of direction. This will be used in the future as a basis for meaningful relations with others. The "stuffed men" or "the hollow people" of T. S. Eliot's poem are bound to become lonely no matter how much they "lean together." The hollow people do not have a solid base from which to learn faith or love. Faith and love take the form of codependence where these two people lean on each other for emotional support and direction but are not individually fortified. When one becomes independent, the other falls hard.

Lastly, anxiety is a threat to self and to faith. Anxiety, the familiar conundrum of our century, intensified during this time of COVID-19. It is even more common and emotionally painful than emptiness and loneliness. It has been pervasive in all of our lives to various degrees. No one who reads the newspaper or browses the Internet needs to be convinced that we live in an age of anxiety. Whether it is the persistent worry that comes from the impending doom of domestic terrorism, the fear of global annihilation, future pandemics, the uncertainty of catastrophic weather forecasts, the downfall of economic stability, or the loss of faith in humanity, I believe that our century is more anxiety ridden than any other period of recorded history since the breakdown of the Middle Ages. Those years in the fourteenth and fifteenth centuries, when Europe was plagued with anxiety in the form of terror of the contagiousness of fatal disease, agonies of doubt about the meaning and value of life, superstition, and fears of satanic powers and sorcerers, is comparable to our own time for different reasons.

Bertrand Russell, a British philosopher, logician, mathematician, historian, writer, social reformer, and political critic of the nineteenth century, once remarked, "The painful thing about our time is that those who feel certainty are stupid and those with any imagination and understanding are filled with doubt and indecision." This can be applied to our time in dealing with anxiety. Anxiety makes reality topsy-turvy. The phrase "age of anxiety" would just as well describe the present time of COVID-19. When we examine our own anxiety issues, we discover that this emotional distress comes from something more profound than the threat of war and economic uncertainty. "We are anxious many times because we do not know what roles to pursue, what principles for action to believe in."[41] We feel lost. The good news is that we can feel lost but not necessarily be lost if we rely on the healthy resources to regroup ourselves by utilizing behavioral routines to combat anxiety or seek support from the faith of others or professional help in therapy. Faith is that human gift that can restore wholeness and security in self.

This is precisely what the present crisis of faith is. Anxiety may occur in slight or great intensity. Anxiety is a roadblock to faith that takes on many forms and intensities. Probably the most common and most stark terror symbolic of anxiety is the threat of death and cessation of human life. Faith doesn't sugarcoat anxiety but provides a lifestyle to combat bewilderment, which is the confusion as to who we are and what we should do. Faith gives us a starting point and a road map where we can strengthen our consciousness of ourselves to find centers of strength within ourselves to stand strong despite the confusion and bewilderment around us. Faith is certain in an uncertain world. Rollo May gives us a very descriptive analogy how faith can be not only a remedy to bewilderment but also an alternative to hollowness, emptiness, and loneliness:

Anxiety, like fever, is a sign that an inner struggle is in progress. As fever is a symptom that the body is mobilizing its physical powers and giving battle to the infection, let us say the tuberculosis bacilli in the lungs, so anxiety is evidence that a psychological or spiritual battle is going on…neurotic anxiety is the sign of an unresolved conflict within us, and so long as the conflict is present, there is an open possibility that we can become aware of the causes of the conflict and find a solution on a higher level of health. Neurotic anxiety[42] is nature's way, as it were, of indicating to us that we need to solve a problem. The same is true of normal anxiety—it is a signal for us to call up our reserves and do battle against the threat.

As the fever in our example is a symptom of the battle between the bodily powers and the infecting germs, so anxiety is evidence of a battle between our strength as a self on one side and a danger which threatens to wipe out our existence as a self on the other. The more the threat wins, the more our awareness of ourselves is surrendered, curtailed, hemmed in. But the greater our self-strength, the greater our capacity to preserve our awareness of ourselves and the objective world around us, the less we will be overcome by the threat. There is still hope for a tuberculous patient so long as one has a fever, but in the final stages of the disease, when the body has "given up" as it were, the fever leaves, and soon the patient dies. Just so, the only thing that would signify the loss of hope for getting through our present difficulties as individuals and as a nation would be a resigning into apathy and a failure to feel and face anxiety constructively.[43]

That hope for getting through our present difficulties and facing anxiety constructively as an individual and as a nation is the power of faith. Apathy and indifference are enemies of faith. This brings us to the crucial point of this chapter—what changes in our culture are occurring or have occurred that make this an age of anxiety, thus enabling the crisis of faith?

I think that the roots of our malady as a culture can be traced back to Rollo May's study of what made the mid-twentieth century a time of bewilderment. He identified five significant losses in our culture that contributes to people losing heart and succumbing to anxiety and weakening their resolve to be autonomous productive human beings.

The roots of self-confusion and bewilderment are due to these profound losses:[44]

1. *The loss of the center of values in our society*
2. *The loss of the sense of self*
3. *The loss of our language for personal communication*
4. *There is little we see in nature that is ours*
5. *The loss of the sense of tragedy*

I contend that these losses are manifestations of our current crisis of faith.

First, there has been a loss of the center of values in our culture.[45] We live in a world where things are always in flux and transition largely due to the progress of technology. What is the center of values lost because of this transition? These are the basic values of individual competition and faith in individual reason. Individual competition that has its roots in ancient Palestine and classical Greece, the birthplace of democracy, voices the conviction that the more a person worked to further one's own economic self-interest and become financially secure, the more one would contribute to the material progress of the community. This has been the case in the US since the Industrial Revolution along with the impetus of capitalism. By the nineteenth century, significant social changes occurred where businesses became corporations and monopoly capitalism thrived so that it became increasingly difficult for people to become successful individual competitors. This caused the vast majority of the labor force and capitalists alike to fit into broad groups such as labor unions or large industries or university systems; otherwise, they would not survive.

It sounds familiar; even today, we have physicians join associations with colleagues of their own specialty to survive economically rather than remain sole providers. This demonstrates the extent this phenomenon has progressed and affected society to the present day. We have all been taught to strive to get ahead of the next person, but today's success depends much more on collaboration with others, which is a good thing. However, the expectation of individual's striving for one's own gain although commendable no longer automatically brings good to the community. Rollo May commented on the unfortunate turn of events that the effects of individual competition exhibit today, "The type of individual competitiveness in which for you to fail in a deal is as good for me to succeed, since it pushes me ahead in the scramble up the ladder-raises many psychological problems. It makes every individual the potential enemy of one's neighbor. It generates much interpersonal hostility and resentment and increases greatly our anxiety and isolation from each other. As this hostility has come closer to the surface in recent decades, we have tried to cover it up by various devices, by becoming "joiner" of all sorts of service organizations...by being good fellows, well-liked by all, and so on. But the conflict sooner or later burst forth into the open."[46]

The second central belief in our modern age that has been challenged has been faith in individual reason. This conviction is centered on the integrity that an individual can utilize both common sense and the use of knowledge as a basis of figuring out things for oneself and use the power of the will to put it into effect. This too became challenged in the nineteenth century primarily by the influence of Rene Descartes's philosophy setting a dichotomy between mind and body. This resulted in human reason seen as separate from "emotion" and "will." Human reason became reduced to intellectu-alistic rationalization used to compartmentalize human personality. Reason was divorced from how the psyche operates with its repressions and conflicts as proposed by Sigmund Freud distinguishing instinct (id)—ego and superego to determine the workings of the human mind. The result of this was the compartmentalization of values and goals not only of the human personality but also for society.

This undermined the unity of the personality that viewed the person as "in pieces" as a puzzle to be put together in studying human behavior. When people talk about personality, they seem to imply that it is made up of compartments by asking—in one form or other—"Should I follow reason, that is, follow my head, or give way to sensual passions and needs, or go with my feelings, or be faithful to my ethical duty in specific life choices?" This challenged the whole idea of individual faith in reason as proposed by Baruch Spinoza's philosophy of the seventeenth century who used the term reason as an attitude toward life in which mind united the emotions with the ethical goals and other aspects of the "entire person."[47] So, the bottom line becomes what had been the center of values of our culture for centuries—the perennial values of individual competition and individual faith in reason became for all purposes obsolete.

What is the new center of values for our culture today? This needs to be identified if faith is to be operative in human lives. This question needs to be answered if human faith is to be viable. The center of values of a culture embraces faith. Just as an individual human being needs to figure out what is one's center of values to become a productive human being so too does society.

Faith cannot be embraced if there are no center of values in society. An example of this is that in Judeo-Christian tradition at the center of faith is service to community and love of neighbor allied with ethical humanism. This center of values has sustained the faith of both traditions to the present day. What is the center of values in our culture today?

A second malady that threatens faith is the loss of the sense of self.[48] If we do not appreciate or accept who we are as human beings with all our limitations, faults, strengths, and potential, how are we to make faith commitments? We need self-awareness to augment our potentials and work on our limitations as human beings. One area of humanity that has gotten overlooked these days that can rejuvenate our sense of self is humor and laughter.[49] One's sense of humor is connected to one's sense of self. Humor not only gives us the space and opportunity to be humbled but also allows ourselves not to be taken too seriously in situations we cannot control. Accepting at times to laugh at oneself is a healthy way of experiencing "distance" between oneself and a problem at hand. Humor allows us to put our dilemmas in perspective. There has been no greater time for this to be true than in this time of COVID-19. When one laughs, it foregoes panic and anxiety so that one is not consumed by the trivialities of life but becomes courageous to deal with the crucial issues at hand with humor not terror.

A threat to a sense of self also arises when one allows to get absorbed and consumed by materialism. Wealth and the need for financial security is part of life. I would be a fool if I didn't recognize that money has power to allow one to obtain what is needed or desired and necessary in living. However, the issue here is not so much the use of money or wealth to establish financial security, but when it exclusively and solely defines self, it becomes problematic for one to aspire to faith. Faith calls for the use of money and the love of people. If I reverse that principle to "I love money to use people," I am in the lifestyle of opulence or decadence not faith.

This makes it difficult to share with others since both are anchored in greed. This is not meant to be a judgmental assessment of those whose lifestyle are of this kind, but it is unlikely when greed becomes the predominant priority in making important choices to define self, faith becomes remote and even nonexistent. It is not money that impedes the workings of faith, but greed that is the love of money and the use of people that sees faith as ancillary and not the ultimate concern. Greed is not just a behavior but a philosophy or mindset in living. As one progresses to choose greed over emotional and spiritual well-being as the ultimate priority, faith is viewed in one's rearview mirror of life. It is not financial investments or financial resources that are detrimental to faith but the sole priority of wealth that makes faith less operative in one's life because it curtails the human act of sharing with others. The aspiration of accumulating wealth for wealth's sake has the potential to drive one to human exploitation, self-entitlement, and self-absorption, which doesn't enhance faith and can never substitute for it.

A third malady of our culture that contributes to degrading faith is the growing tendency to think of the self in superficial and oversimplified terms.[50] By this, I mean so many people judge the value of their work or actions not based on the action or work itself but based on how the action is perceived or accepted by others. It is as though one had always to postpone one's judgment until one check in with one's audience. Thus, we tend to become performers in life to seek validation from others rather than persons who live and act as selves.[51] "Being oneself" goes beyond self-expression or freedom of speech or having an opinion on issues but involves having such a self-awareness of relating to others and self confidence in one's talents that we are secure and certain in our standing in the world. This is what faith in self is about. Faith is certain in an uncertain world. Frequently, self-awareness is lacking not because people lack the intelligence but are so distracted by external stimuli (e.g., acquisition of wealth, power, position, or prestige) that they cannot see the forest because of the trees as the expression goes.

Nowadays, the therapy that is common to empower people to have that self-awareness is called mindfulness. Mindfulness empowers one to walk through the garden of life and be dazzled by the specific colors and take in the unique fragrances of the flowers. Mindfulness is being single minded not simple minded. This means one is so conscious of self that one is not distracted easily away from one's priorities, values, and goals in life. Socrates's precept in ancient Greece voiced, "Know thyself." This does not mean to know all the information about oneself or reasons why we do things we do that takes more than a lifetime to discover but "to venture in the highest human sense that is precisely to become conscious of one's self."[52] It means be true to oneself. It means being honest to who you are and accept yourself for who you are without apologizing. Self-awareness is the first essential step in the process of discovering meaning for the self. This is where faith is found. Faith is born in the self.

The loss of our language for personal communication is another malady that impedes faith.[53] We have already seen how social media has attributed to the loss of human presence; language can be included in this limitation of personal communication. In fact, there are other forms of personal communication besides words: art and music. Paintings, sculptures, and music are the voices of society communicating deeply personal and subjective meanings to others. As intense as the subjective is expressed in music and art by touching the cords of the heart and illuminating the mind, it doesn't necessarily communicate objectively. Truth can be conveyed by art and music, but it is a communication created by different styles and different symbols but what style cannot convey are the thoughts and feelings of the self when articulated or emoted to the world as a matter of fact not necessarily as style.

This objective communication usually comes in the form of the spoken or the printed word not coming from subjective impressions but grounded in facts and data. This language can be embellished but not replaced. Faith needs this language; it needs the language of symbol.

Nietzsche said a person is to be known by his "style," that is, by the unique "pattern" that gives underlying unity and distinctiveness to his activities. The same is partly true about a culture. But when we ask what is the "style" of our day, we find that there is no style that can be called modern… We find a giant like Picasso shifting in his own lifetime from style to style, partly as a reflection of the shifting character of the last four decades in Western society and partly like a man dialing a ship's radio on the ocean, trying desperately to find the wave length on which he can talk to his fellow men. But the artists, and the rest of us too, remain spiritually isolated and at sea, and so we cover up our loneliness by chattering with other people about the things we do have language for—the world series, business affairs, the latest news reports. Our deepest emotional experiences are pushed further away, and we tend, thus, to become emptier and lonelier.[54]

It is unfortunate that we have a very exact vocabulary for technical matters, such as creating a computer program for a diet and exercise plan, but when it comes to human relations, our language limps. When it comes to verbalizing the thoughts of the mind and emotions of the heart, language seems to get lost. A lack of language is detrimental to faith, which needs to be proclaimed and celebrated in word not just in deed.

The loss of relatedness to nature can also hamper our identity of self and in turn have a negative effect on faith. When a person feels inwardly empty, one can experience alienation from nature around oneself. In psychotherapy, I observed that clients who suffered from depression voluntarily deprived themselves of light and warmth. The sunlight of the outdoors and the warmth of temperature were discarded because the person felt cold and disconnected within. Our relation to nature tends to be destroyed not only by our emptiness (depression) but also by our anxiety (lack of mindfulness).[55] Rollo May refers to William Wadsworth's sonnet describing the loss of feelings for nature with the overemphasis on commercialism in the beginning of the nineteenth century where Wadsworth yearns for the mythological creatures of Proteus and Triton of classical Greece. Both figures are personifications of aspects of nature—Proteus, the god of who keeps changing shape and form, and Triton, who is a god whose horn is the seashell and emits music from the large shells on the shore.[56]

> The world is too much with us; late and soon,
> Getting and spending, we lay waste our powers:
> Little we see in Nature that is ours:
> We have given our hearts away, a sordid boon!
> This Sea that bares her bosom to the moon,
> The winds that will be howling at all hours,
> And are up-gather'd now like sleeping flowers;
> For this, for everything, we are out of tune;
> It moves us not—Great God! I'd rather be
> A Pagan, suckled in a creed outworm;
> So might I, standing on this pleasant lea,

Having glimpses that would make me less forlorn;
Have sight of Proteus rising from the sea;
Or hear old Triton blow his wreathed horn.[57]

Lastly, the loss of the sense of tragedy is a malady of our age that not only lessens the worth and dignity of the human person but also infringes upon faith as a human experience. The loss of this sense is basically attributed to the decreased sensitivity of people nowadays to people victimized by crime, natural disasters, family hardships, or personal medical challenges. This has occurred because of a constant exposure of young and old alike to horrific and outrageous events as conveyed on television, motion pictures, YouTube, video games, and the like that desensitized human emotions to the degree of experiencing them as common palatable occurrences. We have become desensitized to other people's pain.

We have become desensitized to people's problems and misfortunes. Rollo May believed that the sense of tragedy is simply the other side of one's belief in the importance of the human individual.[58] If the tragic is not appreciated, there is no need for faith human or divine to inspire change for the better. Recognizing the value of the tragic in life is not pessimism but a realistic approach to realize that life is not always full of "wine and roses" but allows for "the bitterness of vinegar and the pain of thorns" to appreciate, evaluate, understand, and approach one's stance in the world.

What continues to be a disturbing characteristic of our times today that we all are experiencing is that despite the noise and chatter of social media whose sole purpose is to be in touch with people, the quality of our interaction and communication with others can be described as the sound of silence, sound of loneliness, and sound of hollowness. Sometimes the noise of life is so great a distraction we get derailed to attend to and give our energies to what is essential for our living.

The business of life at times can make us deaf, blind, and numb to the priorities we set for ourselves in life. This is not constructive of life nor of faith. As the late John Lennon of *the Beatles* said, "Life is what happens to you while you're busy making other plans." We can be so wrapped up and preoccupied with the agenda of others or the trivialities of our life that we lose ourselves in the process. We lose perspective of reality. These life distractions make the value of self-reflection, mindfulness, and self-giving to pursue meaning from faith experiences impossible and allow it to slip into oblivion.

As we explored, aloneness is healthy for humanity but loneliness not so much. Loneliness results from the experience of hollowness and leads only to human suffering. It may be well to reminisce the lyrics of a famous folk song "Sound of Silence" performed by Art Garfunkel and Paul Simon to describe the nondescript interaction of the generation of the 1960s in response to the social ills of the day, very much like our own day. It reminds us of how faith can be like finding a needle in a haystack if we give in to the silence of loneliness, hollowness, and emptiness:

> Hello darkness, my old friend
> I've come to talk to you again
> Because a vision softly creeping
> Left its seeds while I was sleeping
> And the vision that was planted in my brain
> Still remains
> Within the sound of silence
>
> In restless dreams I walked alone
> Narrow streets of cobblestone
> 'Neath the halo of a street lamp
> I turned my collar to the cold and damp
> When my eyes were stabbed by the flash of a neon light
> That split the night
> And touched the sound of silence
> And in the naked light I saw
> Ten thousand people, maybe more
> *People talking without speaking*
> *People hearing without listening*
> *People writing songs that voices never share*

And no one dared
Disturb the sound of silence

'Fools said I, 'You do not know
Silence like a cancer grows
Hear my words that I might teach you
Take my arms that I might reach you"
But my words like silent raindrops fell
And echoed
in the wells of silence

And the people bowed and prayed
To the neon god they made
And the sign flashed out its warning
In the words that it was forming
And the sign said, "The words of the prophets are written on
the subway walls
And tenement halls
And whispered the sound of silence"

The sound of silence is the crisis of faith.
I would like to conclude on an optimistic note. In the late 1990s, I attended a charity dinner gala at the legendary Waldorf Astoria. Two great former New York Mets were honored for their involvement in local charities—Rusty Staub for his charities in support of families of injured and deceased police officers and Gary Carter for his tremendous work in support of those afflicted with leukemia. I had the opportunity to chat for a few minutes with Gary Carter about what inspired him to establish his foundation. Gary Carter, nicknamed "the kid" for his youthful exuberance, recounted his early crisis of faith. He remembered it began when his mother, who was extremely supportive of his early years as an athlete, was afflicted with leukemia. He remembered that his world was shattered at the age of twelve when his mother died of this illness. In our brief conversation, he remarked that throughout all his success as a major league ballplayer for eighteen years, he experienced in prayer that

"The Lord found him and called him back" from many bleak times in his professional career and life. He was determined never to forget God's presence in his life since he attributed the "Lord's hand" in giving him the skills, energy, and endurance to play sports on the highest level. He told me that since that time of being a professional ball player, his priorities were always his family, baseball, and God who gave him back his life. He remained a devoted Christian gentleman who believed in giving back to people since he was so blessed. In his words to me, "I felt found by the Lord and given a new life to pursue with a new purpose."

It was very difficult to write this chapter since the many memories of the events I recounted were so real, frightening, and vivid in dealing with the pandemic. I leave you with words that we have become so accustomed to that we cannot wait to extinguish them from our memories and vocabulary:

"When we travel in public, we need to exercise an abundance of caution by wearing face coverings."

"We need to spend more time with the folks we live with."

"We need to slow the spread."

"We need to practice social distancing by allowing at least six feet distance apart."

"We need to wash our hands and use hand sanitizer frequently."

"We need to get tested often."

"We need to get vaccinated when our turn comes up."

You and I do not want to hear these phrases again. We want them to be erased from our memories. These phrases bring back vivid memories of a broken and lost world—a crisis we all experienced together, but more than this, it was not only a crisis of everyday living but a crisis of faith. A crisis that has become so profoundly felt by many of us threatened to steal away from us the joy of living.

Chapter 2 Summary

- Crises of faith are as long lived as history itself.
- The crisis of faith always arises and thrives from skepticism of the public's trust in the leadership of governance, organized religious institutions, and even with the medical community.
- The crisis of faith cannot be divorced from the ramifications of the current social, political, religious, and public health upheaval in our nation.
- Faith is a bulwark against falsehood, hypocrisy, disease, human injustice, greed, violence, and human exploitation.
- The crisis of faith demands that we take personal responsibility for our behavior.
- As intolerance toward the liberties and rights of all human lives grows, so too does faith weaken.
- Faith is a universal call that all human lives matter from the unborn to natural death.
- The crisis of faith experienced today is underlined by feelings of bewilderment because one not only lacks the insight in what they want from life but also is uncertain in what and in whom they "believe in."
- Hollowness and subsequent depression exasperated by the COVID-19 pandemic result in the loss of the vivaciousness of life.
- Hollowness is diagnosed as depression not being ingenuous but if not treated endangers faith in humanity.
- Some current trends counterproductive to faith are:
  a) the use of social media to propagate falsehoods or exaggerations about public events or the lives of peo-

ple claiming freedom of speech that instead is "inappropriate reckless license of speech."

b) the use of vitriol where one communicates opinions as unquestionable doctrine so as to alienate others making them seem inferior without intelligent dialogue.

c) the compulsion to use social media to communicate every thought, every feeling, and every behavior daily to receive validation from others to be "politically correct."

d) rewriting or "whitewashing" history in light of current social or political thinking.

- Contemporary challenges to faith are rampant feelings of emptiness, loneliness, bewilderment, and anxiety arising from the uncertainty of our times.

- Faith challenges us to "know thyself" not by understanding why we do what we do but to be true to self.

- Maladies of our time that impede faith are:

  a) loss of the center of values in society.

  b) loss of the sense of self.

  c) loss of our language for personal communication.

  d) loss of the connection with nature.

  e) the loss of the sense of tragedy.

- The loss of the center of values negates faith since values embody faith.

- Sense of self is the individualization of the person where faith is born.

- Language is essential to express faith since the language of faith is symbol.

- Nature as reflective of the world's creation is the theater where faith happens.

- Sense of tragedy is the other side of one's belief in the value of humanity.

- Sense of tragedy gives rise for humanity to utilize faith to inspire change.

- The sound of silence in our culture enabling hollowness is the crisis of faith.

Chapter 3

Symbols of Faith

> As the mind explores the symbol, it is led to ideas
> that lie beyond the grasp of reason.
> —Carl G. Jung (founder of ana-
> lytical psychology)

The term *symbol* derives from the Greek symbolon—*syn meaning together and ballo meaning "I throw"*; placed together, it means
I throw together. This is precisely what a symbol does. It throws
together two realities into a new unity. In psychology, symbol bridges
the gap between the conscious and unconscious world. In mythology, the symbol bridges the everyday world of "now" and the world
as it was in the beginning. In the case of religion, symbol bridges
the divine reality with the human. Since faith deals with the ultimate and is one's ultimate concern whether religious or not, faith can
only be expressed symbolically because symbolic language alone can
express the ultimate.[59] To be symbolic, a word or image must imply
something more than its obvious and immediate meaning; it has an
unconscious aspect of which one is never fully aware.[60]

We tend to use the words sign and symbol interchangeably, but
they are distinct. Unlike signs, symbols not only point beyond themselves to something else but also participate in the reality of that
to which it points. Symbols embody the reality of what it signifies.
Symbols cannot be established, replaced, or altered intentionally for

the purpose of convention or expediency by a society or culture without changing the reality of what it participates in.

Let us take, for example, the American flag as symbol. Some would say a flag is a representation, designation, or even a "sign" of a nation, which seemingly is true; however, in the full sense, the flag not only represents but also participates in the reality that it points to. The American flag is therefore a symbol that participates in the power, tradition, history, and dignity of a people for which it stands. The colors of the American flag: red, white, and blue are not merely color designs of the flag but symbols of the virtues of America: red *symbolizes* hardiness and valor; white *symbolizes* purity and innocence, and blue *symbolizes* justice, vigilance, perseverance. The symbol of the American flag cannot be replaced by social convention unless by some historic upheaval, that changes the reality and identity of the nation. That is why an attack on the flag is considered an attack on its people that it *symbolizes.*

Another example of a symbol is a musical notation written for a composition of music. A musical notation drafted on paper for a score of music is an inanimate sign, but when played by a musical instrument, it becomes a vibrant and melodious sound of life and joy—it is a symbol.

A second distinct characteristic of symbol is that it grows out of the individual or collective unconscious and cannot function without being accepted by the unconscious dimension of our being.[61] This means the shared history of a group of people may produce a symbol that not only represents but actually makes present for the group something of their shared experience. We cannot create a living symbol since we cannot "force" ourselves to be "grasped" emotionally; it simply happens.[62] On the other hand, it is possible for a conventional sign to evolve into a symbol if it produces a response in a group at an unconscious level that actively participates in the power, life, and dignity of the group.

As social symbols arise from the collective unconscious of a group, so does political and religious symbols do the same in that they appear.[63] Symbols like living entities grow and die. Symbols do not grow because people are longing for them and do not die because of scientific or practical criticism. Symbols of faith die because the community no longer produces response in the group where they originally found expression.[64] When the reality identified with the symbol of the life and dignity of a people or group dies, so does the symbol.

Symbols are living entities where signs are inanimate directives. Symbols are intimately tied to the reality they point to. Symbols cannot be replaced by other symbols; their symbolic character is their truth and their power. Genuine symbols are created in several spheres of human cultural creativity such as in the political, social, artistic, historical, and religious realms. It is the latter—the religious realm that best relates to faith for the purpose of our discussion.

Symbols of faith are inherent in the religious realm. It would be beneficial at this point to distinguish between the reality of faith and the institution of religion before discussing symbols of faith. Religion is a social-cultural system of designated behaviors and practices, morals, world views, texts, sanctified places, prophecies, ethics, or organizations that relate humanity to the supernatural, transcendental, and spiritual elements.[65] Unfortunately, there is no definitive definition of the institute of religion. Faith, on the other hand, is a "living out," a lived experience that gives life to beliefs or tenets of a religion. It would appear that faith is inherited in religion, but the converse is not necessarily true. Religion is not necessarily inherent in faith since there are multiple religious expressions and traditions that lay claim to faith.

The reality of faith can even be understood in purely nonreligious terms. The reason is because faith as a human reality is the ultimate concern of one's existence that may not necessarily be defined by elements of religion. A person may be a person of faith without being religious. This does not negate the importance of religious symbols but distinguishes them from the mundane. Religious symbols follow the same criteria as do symbols of faith with the only difference being religious symbols are correlative to a specific tradition of a belief system where symbols of faith are the basic human adherence to one's ultimate concern in life.

Nonetheless, the language of faith is the language of symbol.

If faith is the state of being ultimately concerned as we established in chapter 1, then faith has no language other than symbol. With this understanding, we can discuss different kinds of symbols of faith.

The fundamental symbol of our ultimate concern is God.[66] It is always present in any act of faith, even if the act of faith includes the denial of God. Paul Tillich further clarifies this claim that the fundamental symbol of ultimate concern is God—where there is ultimate concern. God can be denied only in the name of God. One god can deny the other one. Ultimate concern cannot deny its own character as ultimate. Therefore, it affirms that what is meant by the word *God*.

Atheism, consequently, can only mean the attempt to remove any ultimate concern—to remain unconcerned about the meaning of one's existence. Indifference toward the ultimate question is the only imaginable form of atheism. In any case, he who denies God as a matter of ultimate concern affirms God, because he affirms ultimacy in his concern. God is the fundamental symbol for what concerns us ultimately.[67]

With the notion of God, we must distinguish two elements: the element of ultimacy, which is a matter of immediate experience and not symbolic in itself, and the element of concreteness, which is taken from our ordinary experience and symbolically applied to God.[68] God is the premier symbol of faith but not the only one. This is not to reduce the concept of God to solely a symbol, but the symbol of faith is grounded in ultimate concern that traditionally we have identified as God. Other symbols of faith are the qualities we attribute to God (i.e., power, knowledge, wisdom, love, justice, mercy, truth, omnipresence, immanence, transcendence, and righteousness are taken from finite human experiences and applied symbolically to that that is beyond finitude and infinity).[69] Many religious traditions have used anthropomorphic attributes to describe God. The Hebrew Scriptures extensively use these anthropomorphic attributes since no definite name for God could capture the immensity of God's being. God is described as acting in human terms (e.g., in the Book of Kings, God is described as warrior defending his people). Faith uses the human experience of truth, power, forgiveness, mercy, justice, love, etc. to symbolize the content of infinite concern but doesn't posit that this information is about what God did or will do in the future. Faith is the acceptance of symbols that express our ultimate concern in terms of the Divine. Again, these symbols reflect living realities.

Symbols of faith are also manifestations of the Divine in objects, events, persons, and communities, also in words and in writings. These are entities (symbols) considered apart from the secular world classified as *holy* not of themselves but to the degree that they point beyond themselves to the source of all holiness that that is of ulti- mate concern. Holiness is not piety but separating what is considered sacred from the mundane. Traditionally, in the religious realm, many have come to name the source of holiness as God. These holy entities are symbols of faith. For example, in Catholic theology and in some major mainstream Christian traditions, these holy manifestations have come to be known as sacraments. To explain how these manifes- tations (symbols) reflect the reality of the holy, let us take for exam- ple the Christian rite of baptism. The washing of the human being with water not only symbolically posits in words and action that the human being has been cleansed of sin theologically but actually has been made clean in reality. This confirms what the symbol of faith is—the power that affects what it signifies. Faith symbols are more efficacious than mere signs representing belief. Faith is that power that is embedded in the symbol to actually affect what it signifies. Faith is a living reality embracing all of life not a static acceptance of beliefs as we have already discussed in chapter 1.

Another aspect pertaining to the symbols of faith is related to myths. Symbols of faith do not operate in isolation. They are united to stories in the Greek meaning "mythos" ("united to the gods"). Myths are always present in every act of faith, because the language of faith is that of symbol.[70] "The stories of the gods" as prominent in Roman and Greek mythology are usually put into the framework of time and space in discussing the divine-human interactions as told in the annals of different religious traditions throughout history. These stories were regarded as sacred and were embodied in the rituals, morals, and social organization of a culture. It may sound outrageous and sacrilegious that faith is associated with mythology. However, faith is associated with myth in so far as the language of faith is symbolic, and myth is one of those symbolic genres to express faith.

We need to understand that there are two meanings of myths. The first meaning is the ordinary and common usage that is that myths are stories that are untrue used for popular usage, i.e., fairy tales. The second meaning of myth is to refer to stories that may not be literally true but are infinitely true (as confirmed and described by anthropological studies) as far as they describe how life is and how life is to be responded to. It is this second meaning of myth that is operative in understanding how faith is defined by symbol.

These stories (myths) express the ultimate concern in symbolic language. All religious texts have their share of material of mythology present since humanity's ultimate concern uses myth as its expression as told by divine figures and actions in the ageless drama of good versus evil. This is verified by the fact that ancient civilizations attempted to make sense of how the world and universe came to be using myth as symbol. The origins of creation myths as found in the creation stories of the *Enuma Elish of Babylonian myth dates back to the* late second millennium BCE or even earlier to the time of Hammurabi during the Old Babylonian Period (1900–1600 BCE). This pattern was borrowed and became the "blueprint" of the Judeo-Christian and Islam creation traditions as found in the Genesis creation myth. A common hypothesis among contemporary biblical scholars is that these creation myths were discovered along with the first comprehensive draft of the Pentateuch (first five books of the Hebrew scriptures) in the late seventh or sixth century BCE.[71] These myths are true in the sense they describe what life is like whether these stories are literal, historical, or not.

When discussing how myth was used in sacred writings, it is important to understand the following truism: A reality can be true even if it fails the literal or historical test. It is true by the fact that they are based upon what happens in life since these all have been human experience; they often have the same or similar motifs. What is historical is based on what is true; however, what is true need not be historical.

The truth of faith cannot be made dependent on the historical truth of the stories and legends in the sacred texts where faith has expressed itself. Similarly, other disciplines like faith that convey wisdom and truth are not intrinsically categorized as historical but are based upon truth nonetheless, i.e., philosophy, theology, anthropology, and psychology. This is even true of faith. It need not be historical to be taken as truth. This is the rationale of myth being employed as symbols of faith. Different cultures and different times in human history have had different points of view about what life is like, and they have had different cycle of stories to set these forth.[72]

Symbol and myth are forms of the human consciousness that are always present. One can replace one myth by another (broken myth) but cannot remove the myth from human's spiritual life since myth is the combination of symbols of our ultimate concern that we have defined faith to be.[73] It is Tillich's conviction that all mythological elements, whether in the scriptures or other sacred texts, should be recognized as such and are maintained in their symbolic form and should not be replaced by scientific substitutes or philosophical or theological constructs. The truth of faith cannot be confirmed by the latest litmus test of physical, biological, or psychological discoveries, nor can it be denied by them either. Historical truth by its nature is, first, factual truth distinguished from poetic truth of epics or from mythical truth of legend. History describes, explains, and understands the origins and relations and meaning of factual events and records them as distinct from other disciplines of truth. So too, faith doesn't posit factual truth like history but can and must interpret the meaning of facts from the point of view of humanity's ultimate concern.

Again, there is no substitute for the use of symbols and myths. They are the language of faith. Myths do not reduce faith to fairy tale but accentuate faith as the power and fullness of truth about one's ultimate concern. One's ultimate concern is the definition of what faith is. The symbols of faith have genuine standing in the human mind, just as science and art have. Nothing less than symbols and myths can express our ultimate concern. Ultimate concern is not just one's priority but also one's basis for living.

The importance of symbol and myth in the human reality of faith finds its counterpart in the understanding of the human psyche as highlighted by Carl Jung. Jung's system of analytical psychology identified twelve archetypes that are defined as universal, archaic symbols and images that derive from the collective unconscious directing and influencing present behavior.[74] Jung affirmed that primitives did not invent myths but rather experienced them. He saw myths as the original revelations of preconscious psyche as tribe's basic set of stories that constitutes its psyche. Jung said, "A tribe's mythology is its living religion, whose loss is always and everywhere, even among the civilized, a moral catastrophe."[75]

According to Paul Tillich, there is a distortion in the understanding of symbols of faith if one either eliminates or restricts the term *myth* in understanding divine revelation or the realm of the Divine:

One more question arises, namely, whether myths are able to express every kind of ultimate concern. For example, Christian theologians argue that the word "myth" should be reserved for natural myths in which repetitive natural processes, such as the seasons, are understood in their ultimate meanings. They believe that if the world is seen as historical process with beginning, end, and center, as in Christianity and Judaism, the term "myth" should not be used. This would radically reduce the realm in which the term would be applicable. Myth could not be understood as the language of our ultimate concern but only as a discarded idiom of this language. Yet history proves that there are not only natural myths but also historical myths. If the earth is seen as the battleground of two divine powers, as in ancient Persia, this is a historical myth. If the God of creation selects and guides a nation through history toward an end that transcends all history, this is a historical myth. If the Christ—a transcendent, divine being—appears in the fullness of time, lives, dies, and is resurrected, this is a historical myth. Christianity is superior to those religions that are bound to a natural myth. But Christianity speaks the mythological language like every other religion. It is a broken myth,[76] but it is a myth; otherwise Christianity would not be an expression of ultimate concern.[77]

Historical myth is not fiction but the use of history in symbolic language that we understand as myth to be. The Hebrew Scriptures are full of historical myths called midrash, which are fiction but establish a truth about humanity in relation to God. An example of this is seen in the Book of Tobit. This beautiful novella of the love story of Tobit and his wife Anna tells their story of their family living as exiles from Israel after the Assyrian conquest. Through a series of events, Tobit goes blind and sends his son Tobias on a journey accompanied by the angel Raphael disguised as a human. On his journey, Tobias meets Sarah who is afflicted by a demon. Raphael dispatches the demon allowing Tobias and Sarah to marry. They return to Tobit and his wife, Anna. Tobit's sight returns, and he dies old and happy because of God's intervention in their travails. This folktale raises theological questions at the core of the human condition, questions that also find expression with various answers as found throughout the Jewish scriptures such as, why do we suffer?

What are the benefits of being righteous? What is the value of religious tradition? The bottom line is that this tale emphasizes the love, unity, and fidelity of family life. It exults the faithfulness of the love family celebrates together their faith in God and in each other. Likewise, the final Christian book of the New Testament to be canonically accepted—the Book of Revelations (the Apocalypse)—is full of ancient apocalyptic language based upon the symbolism of Greek mythology. It is not a historical book but one that reflects the language of myth to convey eternal truths.

Again, the fact that Judaism and Christianity make use of symbolic language to communicate faith in expressing the history of humanity's ultimate concern that is God is not to conclude that their respective creeds are purely fiction. This is absurd and negates what faith is. It is, rather, that these respective creeds make use of symbols of faith to affirm truths about humanity's relationship with the Divine. Contemporary Judeo-Christian scriptural research over the past century has validated the claim that myth is one of the literary genres employed in the composition of these sacred texts as verified by archeological and anthropological findings. Myths are literary genres of symbolic language to convey divine truths.

There are two types of faith entities that use symbols to identify service to humanity—those that are nonreligiously based and those of religious traditions. Examples of nonreligious based entities that are faith based in serving humanity are The Red Cross organization, UNICEF, and St Jude's Children Research Hospital.

The *Red Cross* is a humanitarian international organization that provides emergency assistance, disaster relief, and disaster preparedness education. The symbol of the red cross is not only its trademark but also a symbol of its faith mission statement to hold human life as premium concern emphasizes the prevention and alleviation of human suffering caused by emergencies of naturally or accidental disasters through the mobilization of the power of volunteers and generosity of donors to alleviate human suffering. Every eight minutes, the Red Cross responds to an emergency via shelters due to natural disasters, provides emotional support to victims of disasters, supplies about 40 percent of the nation's *blood* (*red* cross) supply, teaches skills that save lives in emergencies, provides humanitarian aid, and supports military members and their families. The symbol of red cross is a living mission of service to humanity.

UNICEF (United Nations International Children's Emergency Fund) created in 1946 to provide emergency food and health care to children and mothers in countries devasted by World War II extended its faith mission since to meet the health, nutrition, education, and general welfare of disadvantaged children in 190 countries and territories. Its mission statement is to improve the health care, nutrition, education, and general welfare by safeguarding the rights and dignity of all children (from early childhood through adolescence) especially in emergency situations such as the devastation caused by hunger, war, and the struggles living in refugee camps. The UNICEF symbol features a child being lifted up by the mother overlapping the image of the globe and framed by olive branches symbolizing the hope, security, peace, and joy that UNICEF mission gives to parents and their children throughout the world.

Again, the symbol contains the concrete reality of the mission of UNICEF not just a logo.

St. Jude Children's Research Hospital

St. Jude Children's Research Hospital's mission is to restore a continuum of pediatric treatment and research focused on children's catastrophic disease particularly leukemia and other cancers. With its location in Memphis, Tennessee, it is a nonprofit medical corporation where patients are not charged for their care. It focuses on treating infants, children, teens, and young adults mostly up to the age of twenty-one. The hospital was founded by the entertainer Danny Thomas with help from Lemuel Diggs and Anthony Abraham in 1962 on the premise that "no child should die in the dawn of life," which became its faith mission.

The symbol capturing the mission of St. Jude Children's Research Hospital is the image of St. Jude traditionally identified as saint of lost causes. It is a symbol of choosing faith when all seems lost. The symbol of St. Jude is not just a logo but also a living testament to standing firm in religious truth in the face of an ever uncertain and challenging world. In fact, the child engraved on the St. Jude Children's Research Hospital logo was from a black and white photo hanging on the wall of Debora Williamson's home, one of the few images remaining of her sister, Lisa Smith, a St. Jude's patient who died at just two years old from leukemia. All three entities, Red Cross, UNICEF, and St. Jude's Children's Research Hospital have as their mission statement the protection and service to humanity because of their faith in the value and healing of human life.

Respectively, we can highlight at least three religious faiths among the countless many corresponding to the three nonreligious entities mentioned with the same steadfast faith commitment to humanity. They are Christianity,[78] Judaism,[79] and Islam[80] all by their basic living symbols of faith enhance the value of humanity in light of their understanding of the Divine.

Christianity identified by the symbol of the cross personifies the center and basis of its belief system as grounded in the life, teachings, passion, death, and resurrection of Jesus of Nazareth as documented in the New Testament. Christianity remains the world's largest religion with approximately 2.4 billion adherents in over 157 countries and territories and believes that Jesus is the Christ, whose coming as the Messiah was prophesied in the Hebrew Bible.

A hallmark of Christianity is a living faith in the power of the Risen Christ in response to all human exigencies with the hope of eternal life. The cross is a symbol of the ultimate sacrifice of love made by Jesus Christ to redeem humanity of sin and mirror an understanding of who God is. This understanding of God as taught by Christ leads to change and reform of one's life from sin to grace. This faith in Jesus as Redeemer and Savior has its origins in the one God as pure gift offered to all human beings.

Secondly, Judaism follows the set of beliefs and practices originating in the Tanakh (Hebrew Scriptures) and explained in later texts such as the Talmud. The famous religious symbol of faith for Judaism is the David Star. The six-pointed star of David is a sign based upon David's shield that became the symbol of God's power protecting his people—Israel. The star of David is relatively a new symbol of Judaism popular only in the past two hundred years. The Menorah is perhaps the oldest religious symbol of Jewish faith. It is the seven-branched candleholder recalling the festival of the lights (feast of Hanukkah) commemorating the rededication of the Temple in 165 BCE by the Maccabees after its desecration by the Syrians. The Star of David like the Menorah is not merely a sign but also a symbol of the Jewish faith that tell a story about its people. Similar to Christianity, Judaism centers its faith in the one god and brings to life its faith in living out its feasts in the present lives of its people. In Judaism, such a feast would be the Feast of Unleavened Bread (Passover). These feasts are not only commemorations (signs) recalling past religious events but also a presence of the Divine in the present (i.e., symbols). In Attic Greek, there is a term (*anamnesis*) meaning "reminiscence" or memorial sacrifice. For Judaism, this means that the feasts are not passive recollections of divine intervention but a living celebration of passage from death to life. Such is the feast of Passover symbolic of the passage from slavery to freedom.

When people ritually celebrate the feast, it is a living event that affects their lives now. In this participation of worship, God's saving deeds are made present through symbol. Faith is understood in terms of *Emunah* translated as faith or trust in God, but the term faith alone is not emphasized as with other religions. Emunah refers to how God acts toward his people and how the people respond to him. Emunah is rooted in the everlasting covenant established in the Torah. A traditional example of Emunah as seen in Jewish annals is found in the person of Abraham. On a number of occasions as described in the Torah, Abraham both accepts statements from God that seem impossible and offers obedient action in response to God's direction to do things that seem implausible (cf. Genesis 12–15). Faith could be a necessary means for being a practicing religious Jew, but emphasis is rather placed on true knowledge, true prophecy, and practice than on faith itself. In Judaism, one is to honor a personal idea of God supported by the many principles quoted in the Talmud to define Judaism, mostly by what it is not. Judaism does not require one to explicitly identify God that is called *Avodah Zarah* in Judaism a minor form of idol worship and strictly forbidden since God is understood as transcendent and cannot be limited by attributing names to identify God in human language like other religions do.

The closest the Hebrew Scriptures came to identify God in the response to Moses's request was with the name *Yahweh meaning* "I am who I am" (Exodus 3:14–15). However, this translation is uncertain for it is difficult to decide whether this is a refusal to disclose the name or an explanation of the divine title *Yahweh* revealed immediately afterward. The revelation of the divine name is an early form of the Hebrew verb "to be" (*hwh, hawah*) rather than a noun as one would expect. The phrase, "I am" or "I will be who am" emphasizes God's action in behalf of Israel and not the nature of God as independent being. The name *Yahweh* is the third person masculine singular form of the verb; it translates "he is" or "he will be."[81]

And lastly, in Islam, a believer's faith in the metaphysical aspects of Islam is called *Iman*, which is complete submission to the will of God. One is expected to build faith on well-grounded convictions beyond any reasonable doubt and above uncertainty.[82] According to the Quran, Iman must be accompanied by righteous deeds, and the two together are necessary for entry into Paradise.[83] Islamic symbols of faith are many; however, the star and crescent generally are associated with Islam. The religion of Islam actually does not have a unique symbol as such. The Star and crescent were actually the symbol of the Ottoman Empire that controlled much of southeastern Europe, Western Asia, and Northern Africa between the fourteenth and early twentieth centuries. The five-pointed star reflects the five pillars of Islam that consists of the profession of faith: there is only one god (Allah), and Muhammad is the messenger of God, obligatory prayer (five times per day at specific times facing Mecca), almsgiving or charity (deduct about 2.5 percent of individual income to the welfare of Islamic community), fasting during the holy month of Ramadan; and pilgrimage during one's lifetime to Mecca during twelfth month of lunar calendar.

The governing state of Islam extended the symbol of the star and crescent to its faith. The symbol reflects the foundation of its faith as represented by the five-pointed star.

Similar to Christianity and Judaism, Islam is monotheistic. The crescent moon and star are symbols relating to the greatness of the Creator. The Quran is the sacred text that is the principal source of the daily prayers recited. Again, the symbols of faith in Islam are living testaments of the history of its people's relationship with the Divine. The Five Pillars of Faith are not static or part of their legacy but living symbols of Islamic practice and foundations of Muslim life.

In conclusion, faith is that ultimate reality that drives, empowers, and opens the human heart to the beyond. Faith embodies all symbols religious or not, expressing humanity's ultimate concern of its existence. Faith receives its energy from prayer and silence. Faith is the basis of love. Faith's goal is always service. Faith's interest is tranquility among humanity, unity with nature, and communion with the Divine.

I would like to conclude this chapter with a mantra Teresa of Calcutta wrote to reflect how tranquility of life can be achieved.

> The fruit of silence is prayer.
> The fruit of prayer is faith.
> The fruit of faith is love.
> The fruit of love is service.
> —St. Teresa of Calcutta (1910–1997)[84]

Chapter 3 Summary

- Symbol and sign both point beyond themselves to something else.
- Symbol is distinct from sign in so far as it participates in that reality it signifies.
- Symbols are not conventionally produced by a society but come about from an unconscious aspect of a group that embodies the truth and power of their own shared experience.
- The language of symbol is the language of ultimate concern.
- Faith is expressed in language of symbols because faith is ultimate concern.
- Symbols grow from individual and collective unconscious not intentionally created.
- Symbols grow and die and cannot be replaced by other symbols.
- Symbols of faith differ from religious symbols in so far that they are basic to one's ultimate concern, whereas religious symbols pertain to specific religious traditions.
- Symbols have a power and a truth to manifest; they affect what they signify.
- The basic symbol of faith is identified as God since it is the ultimate concern.
- Faith is the acceptance of symbols that express one ultimate concern.
- There are certain types of symbols of faith that are manifestations of the divine in objects, persons, communities, events, words, or documents designated as holy.

- Faith makes use of myths and symbols since myths are the genre of the language of symbol.
- Myths are compatible with faith since they are stories that are infinitely true because they describe what life is and how life is to be responded to.
- Although myths are stories that may not be historical, nor to be taken literally; they nevertheless express ultimate concern in symbolic language.
- There are no substitutes for myths or symbols; they are the language of faith.
- All religious texts use the language of myth since it deals with the realities of ultimate concern describing divine intervention in the unending battle of good versus evil.

Chapter 4

Faith in the Divine

Called and not called, God will be there.

—Carl G. Jung

Carl Jung understood that everyone is called to attain one's own wholeness. Wholeness lies in the developing dialogue between the self (Jung would refer to as the "God image") and the ego (center of conscious willing and striving).[85] The self for Jung was the divine principle—"the God image" within each psyche that made the soul's individuation possible. Jung understood God's call to each person as a call to the realization of his or her own wholeness for the purpose of individuation. Individualization is a fundamental developmental process to achieve consciousness of self.

In a letter written a few years before his death, Jung spoke about his use of the term God with respect to his experience of an autonomous agent in the psyche.[86] He used the term God in his letters to reflect upon his personal experience of "the Other" throughout his life as realized in dreams, visions, and voices and came to the conclusion that God was no "illusion."[87] Jung's deep conviction found expression as evidenced by an inscription carved over the doorway of his house in Kusnacht near Zurich that reads in Latin, "Vocatus atque non vocatus, Deus aderit," translated "Called and not called, God will be there." Jung said he put this inscription there to remind his patients and himself that the fear of the Lord is the beginning of wisdom. We do not know if Jung was a religious person or not; however, his understanding of the human psyche as having a "calling" testifies to a spiritual dimension present in the human mind. This seems to denote that at best, he was a spiritual person. He attested that the materials in the depth of the psyche cannot be reduced simply to causes in the personal history of each individual but each psyche moves toward the recognition of the role of symbols and myth in the life of the individual to seek the Divine. The archetypes of the collective unconscious of the mind that Jung's theory is known for is where relationship with the Divine is possible. Jung objected to the expression "wholly other" with respect to God. He considered God "one of the soul's deepest and closest intimacies."[88]

These myths and symbols in the collective unconscious have spiritual connotations. As already discussed, myths refer to the stories that are infinitely true how life is and how one is to respond to life. The goal in one's life as far as Jung is concerned is to discover one's myth of meaning in one's life. What is the myth you are living? This is the story (the myth) we find that tells us who we are that must include some explanation of the meaning of human existence in the cosmos. In other words, we need to ask ourselves when we receive "the calling," what is the meaning of our human existence in the realm of the cosmos? We cannot create or invent a myth that accomplishes this for us. It comes rather to us as in Jung's words as "Word of God." We have no way of distinguishing whether it comes from God or not. Everything about this "Word" is known and human, except for the manner in which we are confronted spontaneously and have obligations placed upon us.[89] Jung believed that we are free to choose and follow such inner "leadings," that is, to respond yes to someone or something that makes one certain that existence is meaningful. Following these "leadings" means that one's life is a self-surrender to this goal. However, we cannot dictate what that leading looks like. Jung contends the ego (self) must surrender to this "lead"—"we do not create 'God.' We choose him."[90]

We have now approached "the bridge" of making a life decision. We need to decide—do we cross "the bridge" knowing that we cannot return, or do we remain still or even turn back and not cross over? This is the question we all are faced with at this point of our reflection on faith. We can stop here and end our read and be content to see faith as solely a human reality that motivates us to live good, virtuous, and healthy lives, or we can cross the bridge to see what if anything is on the other side. Is there anything more of faith other than an ultimate concern in the goodness of humanity? Could faith like symbols point beyond?

Does faith empower us to cross over and transition into what is beyond human vision?

To explore this question more deeply, I would like to comment on a similar concern as found in the Christian scriptures. Saul of Tarsus who became Paul, apostle to the gentiles, came to deal with the same crossroads when he was confronted by the Greeks of Athens about making sense of the unknown god that the Greeks were so fascinated about. This account was part of the second of three missionary journeys that took place sometime between c.49–52 CE.

Paul stood up at the Areopagus[91] and said, "You Athenians, I see that in every respect you are very religious. For as I walked around looking carefully at your shrines, I even discovered an altar inscribed, 'To an Unknown God'. What therefore you unknowingly worship, I proclaim to you. The God who made the world and all that is in it, the Lord of heaven and earth, does not dwell in sanctuaries made by human hands, nor is he served by human hands because he needs anything. Rather it is he who gives to everyone life and breath and everything. He made from one the whole human race to dwell on the entire surface of the earth, he fixed the ordered seasons and the boundaries of their regions, so that people might seek God, even perhaps grope for him and find him, though indeed he is not far from any one of us. For 'in him we live and move and have our being,' as even some of your poets have said, 'For we too are his offspring.' Since therefore we are the offspring of God, we ought not to think that the divinity is like an image fashioned from gold, silver, or stone by human art and imagination. God has overlooked the times of ignorance. But now he demands that all people everywhere repent because he has established a day on which he will 'judge the world with justice' through a man he has appointed, and he has provided confirmation for all by raising him from the dead." When they heard about the resurrection of the dead, some began to scoff, but others said, "We should like to hear you on this some other time. "And so, Paul left them" (Acts of Apostles 17:22–18:1).

Paul recognized in the Areopagus at Athens the ecstatic beauty of God's creatures as carved out of stone. The Greeks took pride in the perfect expressions of human form carved in exquisite statues of male and female. By these statues and architectural wonders such as the temples dedicated to Athena and other Greek deities, they sought to communicate with others and to commune within themselves about the wonderful mystery of human nature. Paul used their wonder and fondness of human nature as personified in human forms carved from marble to preach about the One Creator. The mention of the One Creator was Paul's segue to discuss faith as a reality leading beyond our human experience into to a world of resurrected life where divine mystery resides.

Paul in a sense led the Greeks "to the bridge" by his exhortation about the realm of the Divine. Some accepted his message and followed him; others sneered and rejected him, others were undecided and weren't ready, and others hesitated to cross the bridge to the other side. Are we not in the same position when it comes to see faith as beyond ourselves? It is an enormous leap to go from experiencing acts of faith in the human drama as compared to viewing faith leading to infinity, open to divine mystery.

Faith in the Divine whether we identify the Divine as God or "One's Higher power," or "the Almighty," or the "Creator," or "the Ultimate life Source," or the Uncaused Cause, or Ultimate Consciousness has to do with two powerful dynamics. The two dynamics are transcendence and immanence. Both dynamics are complementary attributes of higher life intelligence.

Transcendence refers to higher intelligence that is a completely different kind of substance from and completely independent of the material universe, beyond all known physical laws. Transcendence in the religious experience is a state of being that has overcome the limitations of physical experience. Transcendence can be attributed to a Divine being not only by its omnipresence but also by its knowledge.

A being that transcends is beyond the grasp of the human mind. Its being, presence and knowledge, transcends all and is infinite.

Immanence too refers to a higher intelligence that is inherent, living within, and sustains other beings as its effective cause. Immanence is the balancing concept of transcendence. Many times, immanence gets equivocated with pantheism. It gets associated with New Age or a Star Wars-esque understanding of the "force." The distinct difference is that pantheism claims an impersonal power or force that not only inhibits or sustains everything but ultimately is everything. On the other hand, immanence when applied to a living being is distinguishable from all matter that sustains all but is not everything, nor is everything somehow a piece or part of the immanence of a higher being. Immanence means that this superior being is omnipresent to all living beings and to all matter but not "in" all things. Immanence is defined as a higher being fully present in the physical world and completely accessible to it.

Although transcendence and immanence appear to be opposites; the two are not necessarily mutually exclusive. They are two sides of the same coin. The "coin" is a higher living intelligence that can possess both dynamics at the same time. We had established in Chapter 1 what the essence of being human is—believing and living in relationship with another human being with the capacity to know and love and to be known and be loved. This essence of human existence becomes the point of departure in seeking how the faith journey in our world can transition into the realm of the Divine. Faith as we have attempted to understand is a stance or totally committed lifestyle akin to what it means to be unconditionally and totally human. As we have highlighted up to now, to be totally and unconditionally human is to be divine. This doesn't mean perfection but total and unconditional self-giving. Being human is not a blemish or imperfection of the divine, but when totally actualized is "an image of the Divine." In Christian theology, Jesus Christ is the manifestation of "God became man (human), so that man (humanity) might become God."[92] This is how the human faith experience is a continuum of life into the unknown endless realm of the Divine. The human faith experience with the finality of death is open ended and allows for the possibility of the life continuing into the beyond. For the purpose of discussion, we will identify the beyond as the infinitude of the Divine. Upon the transformation of life with death, one no longer sees reality through the "eyes of faith," but becomes eternal "seeing plainly" what is reality.

Is divine existence "a blueprint" of what it means to be unconditionally and totally human? If so, then it follows that the Divine is the ultimate reality of what it means to be unconditionally human. To be totally and unconditionally human necessitates a personal relationship of knowing and being known—to love and being loved. This is the essence of being human. If we speak of the Divine in terms of relationship, then it is not foreign to what we experience and are accustomed to as human beings. Relationship of human with human follows a continuum of life until death and then, hereafter transforming to a relationship of human with fellow humans in a communion of divine life that is perfected in unconditional love. Traditionally we called this continuum of eternal life heaven. Faith is that conduit that allows one to traverse from the pilgrimage of believing in everyday human encounters into the climax of experiencing full communion with the Divine. We have come to identify this Divine to be God. Love becomes the "connective" and fabric of that communion brought to fruition by faith. Faith becomes the lead to eternal life.

The reality that quickly emerges when we approach the subject of the Divine is mystery. God is mystery. We encounter eternal mystery when we die and enter the divine realm. The divine realm refers to the infinitude of endless beings that are celestial and totally spiritual.

Mystery is a complex reality that has multiple meanings. It can mean anything from the suspense experienced in reading a novel, enjoying a play, or viewing a movie dealing with a puzzling crime or murder to the sublimity of a religious experience. Mystery involves the intangible, the noncorporeal, the incorruptible, the spiritual, and the infinite. Mystery is identified with realities of the beyond, the unexplainable, and realities outside of space and linear time and is the ultimate unknown. Mystery means we can never say the final word about the Divine; there is always more to discover. There is always more to share. There is always more to experience. In that sense, the mystery of the divine invites us never to abandon the endless task of growing to understand the power behind the world we live in, never to abandon faith that power brings us to the precipice of eternity.

Our journey beyond this life through faith brings us to the One who is the ground of existence—we have come to identify as God. Our journey toward God and toward each other in this existence is made along the same road. This road is faith.

This road of faith comes to its climax when it comes to its final destination—God, that is eternal life. Faith allows us to leap into the odyssey of eternity where its final destination is communion with all those who share full life in the Divine. This Supreme being is personal, intimate, and immanent because this divine presence calls for a relationship with other beings. This is the "calling" referred to by Jung in discussing the self as "the God image" on the way to full self-autonomy and liberation. This god is one, undivided communion and relational mystery since the created love emitted is always relational. Faith finds its completion and final resting place in the divine presence where we no longer see through the "eyes of faith" but experience the fullness of eternal life in an unapproachable light.

In Christian theology, the fullness of divine presence is called the beatific vision, which is the ultimate direct self-communication of God to the individual person. The reality of mystery comes into play by the fact that ready or not the most ultimate and final human event that will be experienced by all is death. Paradoxically, faith in the Divine means we must experience death to enjoy life. Faith in the Divine means that I take the ultimate risk accepting death as part of being human so that I can transition into the fullness of eternal life and love. This is what communion with the Divine does—it not only allows human beings to share in divinity but to be divine. This we have come to identify as the state of being we call heaven. Heaven is not a place but a state of being as we are united in communion with the Divine and all those formerly human and celestial who are present in this realm of the eternity. This is what faith in the divine mystery means. It is not a religion but a life—an eternal life.

The life of a human being is destined from a contingent existence to the awesome experience of eternal bliss, light, and love. The divine is the true home and ultimate calling of human who has laboriously journeyed in the faith. Faith in the divine demands that I be open and vulnerable to the experience of death so that I can transition into divine life. This is only true when one is imbued with faith. When faith becomes part of oneself as free gift and choice, there is a power or "vibrant life presence" in that human being operative during the earthly sojourn that makes it not only spiritual but also attracted to and attracted by the divine realm. Traditionally, this is defined as one's soul or spirit. The spirit of attraction is not a "life force" but real, personal, and true presence begotten from relationship. The soul and spirit are not philosophical platonic forms but a life presence called to communion in relationship. Where there is no relationship, there is no need for faith. If there is no faith, relationship with the divine is nonexistent. The state of existence that defines this communion with the Divine and with other beings who are now part of the divine is called heaven.

Discussing what it means for faith seeking the Divine, there are three dynamic symbols to consider: *eternal light, eternal voice,* and *eternal life.* This celestial *light,* piercing *voice, and immortal life* of the Divine are inspired and forged by faith that enlightens, speaks, and energizes the human heart. *Eternal light, eternal voice*, and *eternal life* permeate human existence to attract one to a continuum of life upon death. These are not mythological symbols but divine realities. We may use the language of faith as the language of myth and symbol to appreciate how they relate to our lives in the present, but they forever exist in the afterlife. Faith is both an earthen vessel and passage holding us to and directing us on a path that soars into the beyond. We will define "the beyond" as not necessarily another place in time like that of another universe, but rather as another stratum of existence. This stratum of existence is real and true but not empirically detected or scientifically proven.

John Henry Newman, a prominent English theologian and poet, was an important and controversial figure in the religious history of England in the nineteenth century. He describes the celestial light of faith that enlightens human reason in the following way:

> Lead kindly Light, amid th' encircling gloom Lead thou
>   me on! The night is dark, and I am far from home.
> Lead thou me on!
> Keep thou, my feet; I do not ask to see the distant scene;
>   one step enough for me.
> I was not ever thus, nor prayed that thou
> Shouldst lead me on;
> I love to choose and see my path; but now
> Lead thou me on!
> I loved the garish day, and spite of fears, Pride ruled my
>   will: remember not past years!
> So long thy power hath blessed me, sure it still
> Will lead me on. O'er moor and fen, o'er crag and torrent, till
>   the night is gone. And with the morn those angel faces
>   smile Which I have loved long since, and lost awhile!

Light generally helps us and others to see what already exists in our own person, families, neighborhood, etc. Light brings harmony, good relationships, enrichment, and happiness. Light also induces growth. Plants seek the light. Light brings warmth, love, and new life.

Similar to the enlightenment of faith, the radiance of light activates vision and is a catalyst for action. When we experience light, we can assess the darkness in retrospect. It helps to shed focus on the choices we need to make as we move about in our daily lives. The light always involves making realities present so that we can make good choices. It is here that we can decipher by light's radiance what actions led us into the darkness and unhealthy behaviors morally, psychologically, and socially. It is the same light radiance that enlightens us to reform, change, or convert to goodness and leave the darkness by abandoning unhealthy and self-centered behaviors. The "eternal light" born of faith is that beacon that governs our common sense and grounds us in reality to make virtuous choices. This light gives us new perspectives in making life choices. These choices not only embellish human life but also yearn for eternal life. The eternal light is "the good eye" that is filled with inspiration and able to see goodness and light in the actions and hearts of others. Rather than be annoyed by others' faults, idiosyncrasies, and shortcomings, we need to recognize the good side of people's character. We need to commend them for their virtues, not condemn them for vices, and not imitate the annoying traits of people's self-bragging and boasting. But if we brag, let it be for our suffering, diligence, and efforts to profess our faith despite our human frailties and failures.

The same may be true of the "eternal voice." It is an "internal lead" (to use Jung's words when he speaks of the unconscious) to follow one's own visceral inner calling "beyond one's emotional gut" or instinct. The eternal voice lies in the recesses of the human heart, e.g., falling in love. Or it could be one made in silence and solitude, e.g., a conversion to a specific religious lifestyle or profession of service. This voice is a "calling" and an attraction for one to give heed and "stop in one's tracks" and listen and subsequently follow "one's inner lead." Many have identified this "inner voice" as a calling or vocation. The "eternal voice" could also be a mysterious experience that results in a person's conversion or life reform, e.g., Paul the Apostle's conversion as recounted in the Christian scriptures (Acts 9). The eternal voice needs to be discerned among all the sounds and noise of our busy lives.

I like to describe the eternal voice inspired by faith by quoting one of my favorite baseball sportswriters Thomas Verducci. He wrote a very inspirational reflection called *The Voice of God*, which appeared in a 2019 edition of The Magnificat, a monthly magazine where he defines the voice of divine faith:

"There is a mountain out West I like to climb whenever I visit there. As I climb, I am wishing that when I get to the top, I will have that small space to myself. As much as the view and the rest, it is the silence that I seek. For up there, where the wind whispers, the birds glide without care, and the earth curves away in every direction, it is in the

quiet that I can hear the voice of God…(what) caused me to reflect upon was not just the place and moment but also how we hear God… When Abraham prostrated himself, God spoke to him. There is no mention of anyone with him. Abraham, an old man, lying prone, is the very picture of giving oneself to God. Having quieted himself and his world, Abraham listens well. He does not speak. He learns of this 'everlasting covenant' with God…[As compared to a gospel reading] there is much more noise. Jesus is speaking to a crowd of Jews. They are doubtful. They challenge him when he invokes Abraham and God. Their skepticism grows into intent to harm. They pick up stones to throw at Jesus, who must engineer his escape. Amid serenity, the heart and mind open easily to God; monasteries and retreats, for instance do not have Main Street addresses. It is amid the noise of everyday life, and the influence of crowds and doubters, that it is not so easy. But the voice of God is there amid the noise just the same as amid the quiet. He calls us always, and it is upon us to listen well—mountaintop not required."

Eternal life (the divine realm) is an enormous reality that encompasses both "eternal light" and "eternal voice." It too is an attraction and gravitates the center of the human being from within where faith resides. It drives us beyond our humanity to infinity. Faith tells us this happens. Faith doesn't prove it or document it but points that eternal life is the ultimate concern of human existence. There is a "spark of eternal life" in every human heart, but it needs to be cultivated so that at death it can soar back to its eternal home.

In discussing what is eternal where the faith journey leads and ends, it may be well to consider the true story of Dr. Eben Alexander. Dr. Alexander along with many of his colleague neuroscientists argued that near-death experiences (NDEs) may feel real but are simply fantasies produced by the brain under stress. It was through his own near-death miraculous experience in 2008 with his body lying in a medically induced coma for six days being treated for E. coli meningitis with no hope of recovery that he attests to experiencing visions of the divine (heaven) and the comfort, peace, joy, and warmth of divine presence. As a scientist who doubted the validity of NDEs prior to this experience and a nonreligious person, he couldn't find a plausible empirical explanation why this occurred given the medical state of his brain that it could function at all. He asserted that the coma resulted in brain death and significant damage to the cortex of his brain (outer layer of brain) that regulates memory, language, visual, auditory awareness, emotion, and logic.

Dr. Alexander recalls his condition vividly before his spiritual odyssey:

I didn't have a body—not one that I was aware of anyway. I was simply…there, in this place of pulsing, pounding darkness, language, emotion, logic all gone as if I had regressed back to some state of being from the very beginnings of life…[something] had taken over my brain and shut it down. How long did I reside in this world? I have no idea. When you go to a place where there's no sense of time as we experience it in the ordinary world, actually describing the way it feels is next to impossible. When it was happening, when I was there, I felt like I ("whatever I was") had always been there and would always continue to be. Nor, initially at least, did I mind this. Why would I, after all, since this state of being was the only one I'd ever known? Having no memory of anything better, I was not particularly bothered by where I was…my consciousness wasn't foggy or distorted when I was there. It was just…limited. I wasn't human while I was in this place. I wasn't even an animal. I was something before, and below, all that. I was simply a lone point of awareness in a timeless red brown sea. I came to call it the Realm of the Earthworm's Eye View. The longer I stayed in this place, the less comfortable I became. At first, I was so deeply immersed in it that there was no difference between "me" and the half-creepy, half-familiar element that surrounded me… I had no memory of prior existence, my time in this realm stretched way, way out. Months, years? Eternity? As my awareness sharpened more and more, I edged ever closer to panic. Whoever or whatever I was, I did not belong here. I needed to get out. But where would I go? Even as I asked that question, something new emerged from the darkness above: something that wasn't cold, or dead, or dark, but the exact opposite of all these things. If I tried for the rest of my life, I would never be able to do justice to this entry that now approached me…to come anywhere close to describing how beautiful it was.[93]

Consciousness, ordinarily a product of the brain's frontal lobe, now acted independently of the nervous system and permitted access to a divine reality of the afterlife. Dr. Alexander described his divine encounter:

The journey began with a slowly spinning white light moving up into a valley filled with lush greenery and buds on trees that were blooming. Then I heard a new sound: a living sound like the richest, most complex, most beautiful piece of music you've ever heard. Growing in volume as a pure white light descended, it obliterated the monotonous mechanical pounding that, seemingly for eons, had been my only company up until then… Then, at the very center of the light, something else appeared…an opening. I was no longer looking at the slowly spinning light at all, but through it. There was a whooshing sound, and in a flash, I went through the opening and found myself in a completely new world. The strangest, most beautiful world I'd ever seen. I felt like I was being born. Not reborn, or born again. Just…born… I was flying, passing over trees and fields, streams and waterfalls, and here and there, people. There were children, too laughing and playing. The people sang and danced around in circles, sometimes I'd see a dog, running and jumping among them, a full of joy as the people were…a beautiful, incredible dream world… Except it wasn't a dream. Though I didn't know where I was or even what I was, I was absolutely sure of one thing: this place I'd suddenly found myself in was completely real… I don't know how long, exactly I flew along. (Time in this place was different from the simple linear time we experience on earth and is as hopelessly difficult to describe as every other aspect of it.) There were lots of "and merriment of spiritual beings, souls…lots of joy. And above them, beautiful color clouds and above the clouds, the golden orbs, spiritual beings, with associated music coming down-crescendo after crescendo; pure joy." As I moved through various scenes, I was a speck on a butterfly's wing and someone was next to me: a beautiful girl with high check-bones and deep blue eyes… The girl's outfit was simple, but its colors-powder blue, indigo, and pastel orange-peach-had the same overwhelming, super-vivid aliveness that everything else in the surroundings had. She looked at me with a look that, if you saw it for a few moments, would make your whole life up to that point worth living… "She looked at me with a cherished, loving look," a love purer than any form of love on this earth." His guardian angel didn't speak, but I was able to read her thoughts. Her thoughts were "You are loved, cherished dearly forever. There is nothing you can do wrong. You have nothing to fear." It was the most comforting and reassuring, purely unconditional love beyond description I have ever heard. She also told me through her thoughts, "You are not here to stay. You are going back."[94]

Alexander, who was adopted, said he had some belief in God in his early life, but that ended in 2000 when he reached out to his birth parents, and he was told it was not a good time to connect with them because one of their daughters had died two years earlier. This caused him much grief, anger, frustration, and loss of faith in his natural family, feeling rejected after a lifetime of searching to find them. Months after Eben's recovery, one of his birth sisters Kathy sent him a photo of their sister Betsy who died in 1998. He received the photo in the mail only to discover that the photo of Betsy, this beautiful sister he never met, was the one on the butterfly that he experienced in his afterlife experience.

Alexander describes what he experienced of the divine realm and a glimpse of this taste of eternity:

I saw the abundance of life throughout countless universes including some whose intelligence was advanced far beyond that of humanity. I saw that there are countless higher dimensions, but that the only way to know these dimensions is to enter and experience them directly. They cannot be known or understood from lower dimensional space. Cause and effect exist in these higher realms, but outside of our earthly conception of them. The world of time and space in this terrestrial real is tightly meshed within these higher worlds. In other words, these worlds aren't totally apart from us, because all worlds are part of the same overarching divine reality. From those higher worlds, one could access any time or place in our world. It will take me the rest of my life, and then some, to unpack what I learned up there. The knowledge given me was not "taught" in the way what a history lesson or math theorem would be. Insights happened directly, rather than needing to be coaxed and absorbed. Knowledge was stored without memorization, instantly and for good. It didn't fade, like ordinary information does, and to this day, I still possess all of it, much more clearly than I possess the information that I gained over all my years in school.[95]

Dr. Alexander's testimony of his celestial journey is not scientific proof, nor does it have any empirical basis despite the title of his book, but nonetheless it has "faith proof" that there is a reality beyond us. "Faith proof" I define as an aspect of our humanity that is activated, immortalized, and soars beyond this world to seek its true home. Upon death, this human reality of faith becomes divine mystery. This mystery is more profound and apart from any expression of religion but at the same time is the foundation of all religions. Obviously, I am at a loss of words to speculate about life after death since no one has ever returned from death to tell us what to expect (not withstanding and with all due respect to the Christian belief that Jesus Christ rose from the dead). We can only surmise what the afterlife is by using our imagination along with the beliefs and descriptions given by many religious traditions, metaphysical philosophies, and cultures.

When we discuss the mystery of eternal life, we need to speak of the divine realm. We can define the divine realm generally as the personal territory and topographical expression of a deity. The root of the word divine is literally "godly," but the term varies depending upon what deity one is discussing. In monotheistic faiths, i.e., Christianity, Judaism, and Islam, divinity is often used to refer to a singular God who is central to that faith and has a relationship with its adherents. When the term takes on a definite article—"the Divinity," it is used as a proper name as compared to using the term uncapitalized and lacking the definite article used to denotes "gods" seen many times in the world of mythology. For the Divine to have relevancy for humanity, it needs to encounter the human. There needs to be human awareness and consciousness that this encounter is happening. Divine intervention is a necessary encounter in history as viewed by the powers that accompany it. Transcendence and immanence are those powers. Monotheistic faiths view transcendence and immanence as operative of Divine providence. This acknowledges that the Divine has profound mysterious plan always unfolding in world events. No matter how the term is used, divinity in numberless sacred texts of various religious persuasions, always refers to what is beyond the human sphere, i.e., unlimited in power, endless in knowledge, immortal in existence, and what will be explored later in this chapter—perfect love.

In short, the divine realm is the world of mystery. Without mystery, there is no faith in the divine. Faith as divine mystery is always faith in the divine realm.

Detailing the sphere of the eternal divine presence as a clue to a possible afterlife, we saw in Alexander's journey of soul but not necessarily understand, that before his spiritual odyssey he could not reconcile his knowledge of neuroscience with a belief in heaven, God, or the soul. From his celestial experience during his coma, whether his brain was considered medically dead or his brain functions were "on pause," Alexander is now a physician who believes that true health can only be achieved only when we realize that God and the soul are real and that death is not the end of personal existence but only a transition. Whether the consciousness of Alexander's brain was terminated by his illness or this consciousness took a life of its own independent of the workings of the frontal lobe of his brain, the testimony of Dr. Alexander stands on its own merits.

The three realities of faith in the divine: eternal light, eternal voice, and eternal life tell us that we are in the midst of divine mystery.

In living amid divine mystery, the faith experience is consummated; hope becomes reality, life becomes eternal, knowledge is infinite, and love is forever. Our sole human response to divine mystery is not analysis to determine its validity but only human gratitude as we stand in awe of the depth of mystery. Cicero[96] once commented that gratitude is not only the greatest of all virtues but also the parent of all the others. Divine mystery is not to be proven or historically founded since that is what mystery is not—it is to be held in awe, reverence, and gratitude for the immensity of its presence. Mystery is at the heart of faith. Revelation of what or who the Divine is will not be disclosed until we become part of the divine realm that faith posit to be after human life expires.

Faith in the divine is not solely about a belief system in a Supreme Creator but to come to the final realization that we and others as humans are loved, and it is all about who we are and how connected we all are—the very meaning of existence. We all need to hear each day on this earth that we are loved no matter what our family history and what our current life situation. This is an eternal truth of the mystery of existence. Existentially, we need to hear we are loved because we live in an uncertain, unforgiving, and ever-changing world where life is precious and taken for granted and where time is fleeting. It comes down to "we need to believe that we are loved because in terms of who we really are, where we really came from, and where we are going, we have divine life within." The journey of faith in the divine is the journey and total communion of beings as found in endless love. The journey of faith involves discovering the divine within each of us. "The true value of a human being is determined primarily by the measure and the sense in that one has attained liberation from the self" (Albert Einstein). The self is where faith is born and found. Self grows always limited by human contingences, but it is liberated and freed when it culminates in acts in love. Only faith liberates the self as it sparks and ignites loving action until it finds its resting place in the Divine. Perfect love may not be possible in our present existence, but humans have the potential to strive for it thanks to faith that tirelessly drives humanity to it. This is what faith in the divine is all about. Humanity is transformed to pure love while maintaining its own unique selves. The continuum of life after human death is the eternal communion with the Divine that is the circle of all life.

What does human love look like? How is it experienced? Love is always embodied in human relationships that demonstrate altruism, joy, peace, patience, kindness, goodness, empathy, faithfulness, gentleness, fortitude, trust, fidelity, hope, meekness, mercy, honesty, perseverance, self-affirmation, respect and admiration for the human body, unity of spirit, tenderness, self-giving, forgiveness, tenderness, and generosity.

If these are the attributes of human love, what then is divine love?

It can be capsulized in this line from the Christian scriptures, "God is love, and those who abide in love abide in God and God abides in them" (1 John 4:16). Many religious traditions, spiritual mantras, and metaphysical faiths have similar phrases describing the immensity and depth of love that finds its origins in the Divine.

Our participation in the cosmic process of communion with the Divine calls us to continue as human beings toward self-awareness and toward wholeness of one's consciousness with being in the world. It goes beyond therapeutic mindfulness to a full realization of who we are as human beings, how we are valued, and what is our destiny as citizens of this earth. Faith is a conduit to disclose these truths about our true worth and destiny. Faith's goal is communion with eternal life. Whether this goal is achieved through religious expression or not, it nevertheless is the power, the drive, and the impetus of faith to achieve wholeness—consciousness with the divine realm. In the Christian tradition as with many other religious traditions—the Spirit of God (Holy Spirit) is identified as the vibrant divine presence within each human being upon its existence that develops an attraction during its earthly sojourn to return home to the divine realm. The human finds its origins in "the image of God." It doesn't involve making out of each person a "god," but on the contrary, realizing that within each human being lies the potential of responding to God by bringing that dynamic encounter into consciousness. This was Jung's contribution to what he meant by "wholeness of self"—to bring the encounter with the Divine into one's consciousness.

Ultimately, human love is the fire and soul of faith that brings one to their eternal destiny. Human love, the soul of faith, transforms us from being pilgrims on life's journey to being settlers in the realm of divine mystery as reflected by the ever-popular universal prayer of Francis of Assisi:

> *Lord, make me an instrument of your peace.*
> *Where there is hatred let me sow love.*
> *Where there is injury, pardon.*
> *Where there is doubt, faith. Where there is despair, hope.*
> *Where there is darkness, light.*
> *Where is sadness, joy.*
> *O Divine Master, grant that I may not so much seek to be*
> *consoled as to console*

to be understood, as to understand.
To be loved, as to love.
For it is in giving that we receive
and it is in pardoning that we are pardoned
and it is in dying that we are born...to eternal life.[97]

Chapter 4 Summary

- Carl Jung defined the self as the divine principle that strives to attain one's wholeness—self-individuation.
- Faith in the Divine recognizes the reality of a supreme life presence—transcendent and immanent.
- Transcendence denotes that this supreme life presence is independent of the material universe and not governed by the laws of physical science.
- Immanence denotes that this supreme life presence is inherent, living within, and sustains all beings as an effective cause.
- Transcendence and immanence are complementary divine realities in humanity's attempt to give expression to the existence of a supreme spiritual higher intelligence.
- Although the divine supersedes the human, the Divine is the "blueprint "of what it means to be unconditionally and totally human.
- Divine existence and the human experience are all about the dynamics of relationship.
- Relationship to the Divine and to the human as well necessitates that the core of one's being (self) is to know and to love the Other, to be known and be loved by the Other.
- The Supreme being like that of the human exists in relationship.
- This Divine presence is personal, intimate, and eternal not a life force of the universe.
- Faith in the Divine necessitates a continuum of life leading to full communion with God.
- When we adhere to faith in the Divine, we need to acknowledge the reality of mystery.

- Mystery is a reality that is endless, incorporeal, not the final word on existence, always more to discover about being, always more to share, more to experience, an existence of infinite possibilities, and beyond the human psyche.
- Without mystery, there is no faith in the Divine since faith in the Divine is mystery.
- Faith in the Divine paradoxically necessitates death as a life transition to eternal life.
- Faith beckons the self to transcend upon death to its ultimate eternal continuum of life.
- The symbols of faith in divine mystery are eternal light, eternal voice, and eternal life.
- Eternal light is a beacon of enlightenment, or "inner vision" ignited by faith to give inspiration and perspective to one's life choices.
- Eternal voice is the "inner calling" or "internal lead" that attracts one's being to be moved and converted by Divine presence to that that is good and truthful.
- Eternal life embodies both the symbols of *light* and *voice* in providing the spirit of one's being with the fullest knowledge of all truth, the comfort of limitless goodness, and the communion of endless love with all of life.
- Faith in the Divine necessitates a "wholeness of self," that is, a full and clear consciousness of self upon encountering the source of all life—God.
- Human love is the fire and soul of one's faith in the earthly sojourn that brings one to full communion and full realization of the Divine (beatific vision).
- There is a "spark of eternal life" in every human heart that needs to be cultivated in this life so that at death, it can soar back to its eternal home.
- Faith is the "road map" to cultivate and harness that "spark of eternal life" inherent in the human heart that leads to the Divine.

Chapter 5

Divine with a Human Face

> The relation to a human being is the proper metaphor for the relation to God... A person cannot approach the divine by reaching beyond the human. To become human is what this individual person has been created for.
>
> —Martin Buber

When we try to find words to express something important to us—like how we felt when "we fell in love"—we are speechless due to the limitations of language. The perils of language dishearten our efforts to express ourselves as clearly as possible, all the time aware that our words seem to diminish the truth we are struggling to make known. Such is the case of articulating faith in the Divine. We falter. We stammer. We keep on trying by saying to ourselves, "If only I had the right words," or "Well, it's something like..."

As T. S. Eliot observed,

> *It's strange that words are so inadequate.*
> *Yet, like the asthmatic struggling for breath*
> *So, the lover must struggle for words.*

Many times, when we want to explain anything, we must speak in metaphor or similes. All good communication and teaching address the unknown by starting with what is known. This is truly the case when we attempt to make sense out of the mystery of faith in the divine. We need to uncover what is at the heart of faith as it relates to the human journey before we can appreciate the ramifications of "believing in" the Divine. The common denominator operative for both human and divine realities is relationship. We established in chapter 1 that faith can only be meaningfully understood solely in terms of human relationship. The same can be said of faith in the Divine. Faith in the Divine involves not only believing in the existence of the "Other" beyond the self but being committed to seeking a relationship to know and love that "Other" and allow that "Other" to reciprocate.

In this case, that "Other," I strongly suggest, is a divine personal being. Divine because this "Other" is both beyond our world (transcendent) and exists in the matrix of our world (immanent). This being is personal because relationship is at the core of the Divine's existence—being because the Divine is not merely an energy or cosmic force but a subject (an I) that creates, inspires, knows all, is a source of love, and can be known and be loved.

Relationship is the cornerstone of the human seeking a connection with the Divine. The dynamics of relationship puts a human face on the Divine. The pivotal word here is connection. We need connection to make relationships work. Whether the connection among humans is physical, emotional, social, sexual, cerebral, or spiritual, the only reality we are all familiar with no matter what the type of connection, is relationship. Relationship is the connection that makes life happen and have meaning. This is the starting point of our exploration about how the human relates to the Divine. Just as we get to know the unfamiliar through the familiar, we get to know the Divine, the unfamiliar through the familiar. We do this through the familiarity of our human relationships.

Relationship is pivotal in giving us some clue about how faith relates to the mystery of the divine. We have already explored how faith as human reality works in relationships and how precious and fragile it is. Our human psyche cannot comprehend nor grasp the mystery of faith in the Divine since ordinarily we have no conscious direct experience of the Divine. Human relationship that is the familiar can help us put a human face on the unfamiliar. I suggest that by using the analogy of how human relationship works we can surmise how a human connection with the Divine is possible.

One of the most accomplished thinkers of the twentieth century who tackled how relationship can be used to put a human face on the divine was the Austrian-Israeli religious existential philosopher Martin Buber.[98] One of the major themes of his book *I and Thou* contends that human life finds its meaningfulness in relationships. In Buber's view, ultimately, all our human relationships bring us into relationship with God whom he describes as the *Eternal Thou*. Buber suggested that the existence of humans is defined by two-word pairs—the *I-It* and the *I-Thou*. The I-It relation refers to the world of experience and sensation. It is the world viewed as individual objects and the distinctions among these entities.

Fundamentally, it refers to the world we experience. An example of an I-It relation would be that if in a human relationship, lovers find self-fulfillment and self-growth as a projection of themselves in each other. This is not authentic love but merely falling in love with the experience of "falling in love." In this case, the I (the subject) objectifies the other human (as it) in Buber's interpretation of human existence. It is an I-It relation. We can extend this notion in religious matters too. The I-It relation would look like that if we abstract the notion of God exclusively in terms of the ultimate life principle or cosmic power or energy force, we have reduced the definition of who God is to an object (as it). This would be reducing the relationship between God (the Divine) and the human as I-It relation. All I-It relations have to do with describing entities as discrete objects drawn from a defined set of entities, e.g., he or she is defined as what makes them different from other, he's or she's. Here the objects can be measurable by their characteristics such as facial appearance, color of hair, the sound of their voice, their height, or their age, etc. I can have a distinct relationship of this type with as many he's or she's in one lifetime that all would be referred to as an I-It relation. I-It relations are not bad but are only functional and ephemeral to get through life. They are not life giving. I-It relations solely help me navigate through human experiences to help me get to my goals.

On the other hand, the *I-Thou (you)* relation exclusively describes the world of relationship. It is a sacred and unbreakable bond between two subjects: between two "I's." Here I (the subject) doesn't objectify the other ("it") but is imbued with the living presence of the Other (Thou). I-Thou relationships are living and dynamic sustained in the spirit and mind of an "I" (the subject) for however long the feeling or idea of relationship is the dominant mode of perception.

The essential characteristic of an "I-Thou" relation is that it is solely and foremost a "dialogue of presence" of I "with the Other." There is no in-between. Presence is an existential bond of souls created by two living "I's" in the "now" not for any other purpose than being with each other. This is the primary characteristic of this type of relationship. It is solely an existential reality with no other purpose than "to be for the Other and the Other to be for the subject." It demands full concentration and mindfulness. This means to live fully in the present, exclusively in the here and now, and not to think of the next thing to be done, while I am doing something right now—that is being with another. In psychological terms, it is the height of one's mindfulness.

It is the I-Thou relation that is the point of departure for exploring the relationship of the human with the Divine. In its purest form, the *I-Thou relation* is between humanity and the Divine. It becomes the model for all human relations. The "inborn thou" (the natural self) is expressed and realized in each relation, writes Buber, but it is consummated only in the direct relation with the Eternal Thou (God), which Thou by its nature cannot become an *it*.

Buber's philosophy of existential personalism was influenced by Hasidic mysticism that purported that humanity could achieve an intimate personal relationship with God through intimate relationships with fellow human beings. The Hasidic ideal, according to Buber, emphasized a life lived in the unconditional presence of God, where there was no distinct separation between daily activities and the religious experience. In this understanding, living of itself is a spiritual or religious experience that is beyond mere existing. There is a dynamic, life-giving presence in humanity that goes beyond existence. This presence personifies and allows the human to become an "image" of the Divine. It sounds similar to the traditional religious belief of the existence of the soul or spirit in the body.

Many times, we have heard the expression "life is a prayer." This originated with the spirituality and monastic rule of St. Benedict of Nursia who founded Western monasticism and insisted that in the presence of God, all work is prayer (Latin: ora et labora), which had as its foundation everything you do is prayer. There is no dichotomy between spirituality or religion and the experience of living. Similarly, for Buber, religion was an experience in living where humanity is given the opportunity and challenge to utilize responsibility to achieve self-truth, justice to do good toward others, freedom to aspire to one's destiny, and love in developing a relationship with the Other. Religion is not merely a rule of conduct by rather a "spiritual experience of life" where the self seeks the Divine.

For Buber, the Other can be identified as one of the three spheres of existence: nature, another human being, a spiritual entity or ultimately—God. For our purposes, we will define this Thou or Other as God.

Buber not only viewed God as the great mystery of existence totally Sacred and Holy but also insisted that God was wholly the same with us. In Buber's words, God is "nearer to me than myself," i.e., nearer than my "I" and cannot be spatially located in the transcendence beyond things or the immanence within things. Buber called God the *Eternal Thou*.

Buber uses the analogy of human relationships as a basis to understand the I-Thou relationship:

The I-Thou relationship allows humanity to encounter itself and be so introspective and transparent to self that it is alleviating all pretensions, self-vanities, and allusions. It is a spiritual reality that embodies the whole of one's being.

Humanity discovers its own distinctiveness and identity only through I-Thou relationship with others [hence the common expression "We learn who we are by the quality of our relationships with others"]. The I-Thou relationship is so intimate that it not only validates the talents, dignity, and goodness of other human beings but lives a life congruent and in harmony with the other. The I-You (Thou) relationship is characterized by mutuality, directness, present-ness, intensity, and ineffability.

As compared to the I-It relationship that objectifies humans, the I-Thou relationship describes the between of I and You as a bold leap of faith into the experience of the other while simultaneously being transparent, present, and accessible. The Thou (You) has no borders. The Thou (You) possesses nothing; does "not have" something, has nothing; rather solely stands in relationship. When humanity experiences the world, i.e., people, places, things; humanity brings back from these realities some knowledge of their condition we call experience. However, it is not the experience alone that brings the world to humanity but only bring the world of "It" to humanity. The world of itself does not participate in the world but allows itself to be experienced by the human. The world as experience belongs to I-It reality of existence, which is impersonal, imperfect, and objectified. The I-Thou (You) establishes the world of relations.[99]

Buber further explores the I-Thou relationship in terms of the depth, transparency, harmony, and mutuality of human relationship.

When I confront a human being as my You (Thou) and speak the basic word I-You to them, then he/she is nothing among things, nor does he or she consist of things. He or she is no longer he or she, limited by other he's or she's, as a dot in the world grid of space and time, nor a condition that can be experienced and described, a loose bundle of named qualities... Not as if there were nothing but he or she, but everything else lives in his or her light. Even as a melody is not composed of tones nor a verse of words, nor a statue of lines—one must pull and tear to turn a unity into multiplicity—so it is with the human being to whom I address as You from him or her the color of his or her hair or the tone of his or her speech or the color of his or her graciousness; I have to do this again and again; but immediately he or she is no longer You... I do not find the human being to whom I say You in any Sometime and Somewhere. I can place him or her there and have to do this again and again, but immediately he becomes a He or a She, an It, and no longer remains my You. The human being to whom I say You I do not experience. But I stand in relation to him or her in the sacred basic word... The relation to the You is unmediated. Nothing conceptual intervenes between I and You, no prior knowledge, and no imagination; and memory itself is changed as it plunges from particularity into wholeness. No purpose intervenes between I and You, no greed and no anticipation; and longing itself is changed as it plunges from the dream into appearance. Every means is an obstacle. Only where all means have disintegrated encounter occurs.[100]

From this description, we can conclude that human presence to another (I-Thou) is the sole fabric, soul, and primary characteristic of human relationship. It is not extracting knowledge from the world in experiences "he," "she," or "it," but sole presence that is at the essence of relation with the Other that creates mutuality, harmony, and spiritual unity.

If "Thou" is used in context of an encounter with another human being, the human being is not merely he, she, or bound by anything. You do not experience the human being as distinct entity; rather you can only relate to him or her in the uniqueness and sacredness of "presence." The I-Thou relation cannot be explained; it simply is. It is solely and exclusively existential. The closest example I can think of to describe this is—lovers who are present to each other are soul mates. They are distinct but as individuals unified in one heart, one mind, and one being without words or action. They are being for each other. Lovers look at each other without words but stand present for each other. Nothing intervenes in the I-Thou relationship. It is not a means to some goal or object, but a definitive relationship involving the whole of one's being. As we admitted earlier in discussing the limitations of language, language cannot capture the depths and riches of the relationship of two subjects. This presence is likened to soul with soul or heart with heart with no linguistic interaction or explanation needed.

The Divine enters our discussion of relationship because the origin of being itself is the Divine. The world of being is beyond us whether we wonder about the galaxies of endless universes or we are in awe of the intricacies of the human body. Near or far, we cannot escape the reality of being. In the large scheme of existence, human birth remains awesome, and the finality of human death remains hauntingly mysterious. Being is the very ground of existence. The Divine is creator of that being. "Big Bang" theory or not, God is.

It is through such an authentic encounter with the divine presence that humanity can be open and be transformed by its power. This power of presence is greater than any human subject unfolding continuously in a dialogue of spirit with another. The I-Thou relation is that encounter where humanity encounters the divine presence and becomes divine. In traditional religious language, we call this encounter heaven.

A second important characteristic of relation is reciprocity. Reciprocity is always a give-and-take. Reciprocity means that relationship is always a constant, never a "trade-off" but a full "buy-in." The mutual presence of I-Thou is a two-way street. For any human relationship to be validated, it needs to be reciprocated. The plight of the human condition is that there is no relationship that has a reciprocity factor of 100% since no human being nor any couple can actualize their connection perfectly. This relationship of I-Thou is best manifested in the sacred experience of human friendship. Here the individual perceives an affinity with the Other, i.e., a friend. One is attracted to "a sort of likenesses to oneself." This doesn't mean that the friend looks physically like us or has the same personality as us, but a spiritual bond instantaneously happens with the encounter. The I-Thou relation just happens. This attraction comes into view many times because of the other's goodness, kindness, compassion, empathy, common interests, transparency, and mutuality in the initial interaction. This reciprocity exhibited by the fidelity of human friendship is succinctly described in the Jewish scriptures as such:

A faithful friend is a sturdy shelter he (she) that has found one has found treasure. There is nothing so precious as a faithful friend, and no scales can measure his(her) excellence. A faithful friend is an elixir of life, and those who fear the Lord will find him(her).

Whoever fears the Lord directs his (her) friendship aright for as he (her) is, so is his (her) friend also (Sirach 6:14–17).

We conclude from this that faithfulness as the core of human friendship is the elixir of "the presence" of one to another. The fidelity of human friendship is the reciprocity of relationship modeled upon the I-Thou relation of the Divine to the human. However, the power of human presence in friendship can never be completely exhausted because we as humans are not perfect beings. Only a Divine being seemingly would be capable of this task.

Seeking the divine in the human is what friendship purports to accomplish. This doesn't deify humanity but only enthralls one into a movement of spirit to full union with the Divine. This is the only communion where complete reciprocity is actualized. This inner drive, attraction, or hunger to seek the Other is the resilient movement we understand faith to be. This is how faith as human reality evolves into the relentless drive into the mystery of the Divine. When one enters this mystery, faith has attained its mission, and eternal life is now ever-present.

Who then can provide perfect reciprocity? This opens the possibility of human dialogue with the Divine—would God be that Eternal Thou to ensure that perfect reciprocity? What seemingly opens the door for a conversation of faith in the Divine presence is the offer to humanity of a life of total reciprocity, intense presence, mutuality, harmony, and communion initiated by a supreme personal being. This would be Buber's Eternal Thou. This relationship would be a "blueprint" for all human relationships engaged in faith journeys.

Following this logic, the ultimate Thou is God. In the I-Thou relation, there are no barriers or boundaries. This enables us to relate directly to God. God is ever-present in human consciousness because of God's immanence also manifested in music, literature, religion, and other artistic forms of culture. When God is manifested in these forms of culture (objectifications), the Eternal Thou is now addressed as It, since God is spoken about as object not spoken directly as "I." That is exactly the difference between experiencing the sheer presence of relationship and describing the relationship objectively that religion always needs to be vigilant. There is no world that disconnects humanity from God when I-Thou relation is operative. Therefore, God is the worldwide relation and foundational ground of all relations whether in nature, with humanity, or with the spiritual realm.

To use the analogy of human friendship to understand the relationship of humanity with the Divine, Maurice S. Friedman, an interdisciplinary, interreligious philosopher of dialogue and biographer of Martin Buber, describes the relationship of humanity with the Divine (Eternal Thou) as an infinite dialogue of presence:

To go out to meeting the Eternal Thou, a human being must have become a whole being, one who does not intervene in the world and one in whom no separate and partial action stirs... "He who enters the absolute relation is concerned with nothing isolated anymore." He sees all things in the Thou and establishes the world on its true basis. God cannot be sought; He can only be met... It is foolish to seek God, "for there is nothing in that He could not be found." The meeting with God is a finding without seeking, a discovery of the primal, of origin. "The finding is not the end but only the eternal middle, of the way. God is the Being that is directly, most nearly, and lasting over against us, that may properly only be addressed, not expressed."... Solitude is necessary for relation with God. It frees one from experiencing and using, and it purifies one before going out to the great meeting. But the solitude which means absence of relation and the stronghold of isolation, the solitude in which man conducts a dialogue with himself, cannot lead man to God... He who has relation with the Eternal Thou also has relation with the Thou of the world. To view the religious man as one who does not need to take his stand in any relation to the world and living beings is falsely to divide life 'between a real relation with God and an unreal relation of I and It with the world. No matter how inward he may be, the 'religious' man still lives in the world. Therefore, if he does not have an I-Thou relation with the world. He necessarily makes the world into an It. He treats it as means for his sustenance or an object for his contemplation. "You cannot both truly pray to God and profit by the world. He who knows the world as something by which he is to profit knows God also in the same way."[101]

The opposing stance to "being presence to the Other" is isolation, self-absorbance, and alienation that in turn objectifies any relation to the Other. So too like the I-Thou relation, love is a subject-to-subject relationship. Love is not merely a disposition of emotion toward another or a relation of subject (I) to object (it) but rather a relationship where both subjects immerse themselves in a unity of beings. The concentration needed to be present to another must be exhibited most of all by people who love each other. This unity of beings is not empirically measurable like one's behavior or personality but an intangible presence of the unity of souls.

Love is not only a condition encompassed by the I-Thou relation, but it is a "presence" and basis for interpersonal creativity that is at the heart of human relationships. So, the third characteristic of human relationship is interpersonal creativity that is shared by two human beings.

Love drives lovers to transform themselves from self-interest to being self-gift to each other. Love is the dynamic interaction of the I with the Thou (You) where both beings so crave for unity with each other that they give of themselves without reservation. They thrive in the unconditional dimension of their love for each other.

Love's drive goes beyond the physical but encompasses the emotional and spiritual as well. When it encompasses the spiritual, it mobilizes the movement of faith to integrate all the self's talents and abilities and reaches out to others seeking communion. Ultimately this union is with the Divine and all beings who share in the divine realm of existence.

The goal of this interpersonal creativity that causes each person to experience self-transformation is full communion and eternal bliss. This is the communion that humanity aspires to when it "buys into faith." Love becomes the elixir and ultimately the soul of one's being that aspires unity with the eternal Other. Love becomes the unfathomable "living stuff" that activates faith to navigate life's journey to attain one's eternal destiny. For those whose faith is solely in humanity, it becomes the serenity and satisfaction of making a difference in this world. For those who believe in the Divine, it becomes the eternal peace of afterlife. Faith in both scenarios played an instrumental part of one's destiny.

The only path to true knowledge and love is a communion of beings where one knows and loves and in return is known and loved by the Other. Love is that living presence that makes this communion of life possible. The only difference is that with humanity, love is time bound and transient, whereas with the Divine, it is endless and eternal. Presence in the act of loving—the giving of self to the Other—is the dynamic that actualizes communion. In the human sphere, communion can take many forms: communion of companionship in friendship, communion of bodies and hearts for lovers, communion of wisdom for those who mutually pursue knowledge, communion of life and love for the married or committed couples, and communion of trust and sharing in families. The revelation of truth and knowledge of self and others is what love unfolds. Both knowledge and love are catalysts for interpersonal creativity that takes place in authentic relationships.

If we take a step further, we will see that this communion of love with the Divine leads to full knowledge and truth of self. In the Divine, one comes to full consciousness of self. There is a term in biblical Hebrew that concisely defines this type of love called *hesed*. This term was used in the Jewish scriptures to define the love relationship between God and Israel loosely translated in to mean "steadfast love" or "faithful love." Its meaning is more visceral than these English translations.

This love is understood in the context of a covenant that you make with another person. The concept of covenant was not only legally binding in Jewish tradition, but one made "in blood"— meaning giving oneself fully, with love and compassion to another. It connoted a superlative commitment made by one to another in loving/kindness. This concept *hesed* appears in the Torah more than 190 times and is one of the most beautiful words in the entire Bible expressing this premier relationship. It is through this loving kindness to others that one finds oneself. Love results in self-knowledge.

The fourth characteristic of relationship is seen in the connection between knowledge and love. Erich Fromm in his book *The Art of Loving* describes the relationship of knowledge and love this way:[102]

The only way of full knowledge lies in the act of love: this act transcends thought, it transcends words. It is the daring plunge into the experience of union I have to know the other person and myself objectively, in order to be able to see one's reality or rather, to overcome the illusions, the irrationally distorted picture I have of another. Only if I know a human being objectively, can I know one in one's ultimate essence, in the act of love... The experience of union, with man, or religiously speaking with God, is by no means irrational. On the contrary, it is as Albert Schweitzer[103] has pointed out, the consequence of rationalism, its most daring and radical consequence. It is based on our knowledge of the fundamental, and not accidental, limitations of our knowledge. It is the knowledge that we shall never "grasp" the secret of man and of the universe, but that we can know, nevertheless, in the act of love.[104]

We heard many times that knowing is loving and loving is knowing. In the Biblical sense, "knowing" means full carnal communion that is shared by two beings who are lovers. Although authentic relationships may include but transcend the mere physical, the more we know someone whom we are in relationship with, the more we love them and vice versa. This is at the essence of authentic relationship—full union. Knowledge of others becomes the dyad of loving. In turn, this knowledge becomes the catalyst of self-knowledge and love of self as we love others.

A fifth characteristic of the fabric of human relationship is complementarity. Complementarity involves the polarity of opposite entities in the world not necessarily the attraction of opposites. In the natural order, this complementarity would be seen as the earth being watered and refreshed by the rains of the atmosphere; the cycle of the dying of living things in nature in winter with the promise and hope of resurrection in the spring; the springing forth of new life in nature from the natural processes of penetration and receptivity, matter versus spirit; and the flowing river versus the immensity of the ocean.

When this polarity is applied to humanity, it would look like the complementarity of one human being to another human being, traits of masculinity complementing femininity, birth versus death, planting versus harvesting, building versus destroying, weeping versus laughing, mourning versus serenity, embracing versus distancing, seeking versus losing, silence versus speaking, love versus hate, and war versus peace. So, too, complementarity is seen in the relationship of the human with the Divine, e.g., perfect vs. imperfect, infinite versus finite, and Creator vs creature.

An ancient Muslim poet and mystic, Rumi, described the polarity and complementarity in nature and among humans with a perspective to the Divine:

> *Never, in sooth, does the lover seek without being sought by his beloved. When the lightning of love has shot into this heart, know that there is love in that heart.*
>
> *When love of God waxes in thy heart, beyond any doubt God hath love for thee.*
>
> *No sound of clapping comes from one hand without the other hand.*
>
> *Divine Wisdom is destiny and decree made us lovers of one another. Because of that fore-ordainment every part of the world is paired with its mate.*
>
> *In the view of the wise, Heaven is man and Earth woman:*
> *Earth fosters what Heaven lets fall.*
>
> *When Earth lacks heat, Heaven sends it; when she has lost her freshness and moisture, Heaven restores it.*
>
> *Heaven goes on his rounds, like a husband foraging for the wife's sake. And Earth is busy with housewiferies; she attends to births and suckling that which she bears. Regard Earth and Heaven as endowed with intelligence since they do the work of intelligent beings. Unless these twain taste pleasure from one another, why are they creeping together like sweethearts?*
>
> *Without the Earth, how should flower and tree blossom?*
> *What, then would Heaven's water and heat produce?*
>
> *As God put desire in man and woman to the end that the world should be preserved by their union. So hath He implanted in every part of existence the desire for another part. Day and Night are enemies outwardly; yet both serve one purpose Each in love with the other for the sake of perfecting their mutual work*
>
> *Without Night, the nature of Man would receive no income, so, there would be nothing for Day to spend.[105]*

For Rumi, love is the interpersonal creativity that bridges all polarities both in nature and in humanity. When we're in the state of love, we attract what we desire. Love underlies the complementarity in the world to balance polarity.

This is that harmony that dictates the relationship of humanity with the Divine. Complementarity is at the soul of relationship. It is the yin and the yang of life that in Chinese philosophy and religion—two principles that are seemingly opposites—i.e., one the negative, dark, and feminine (yin) and the other one the positive, bright, and masculine (yang)—whose interaction influences the destinies of creatures and things including relationships.

Complementarity is where opposite realities are seen as interconnected and counterbalancing. It is not so much that opposites attract; rather opposites are in balance and complement each other when the Divine meets the human. An example of this complementarity is evident in Christian belief where Jesus Christ is seen as the human face of the Divine. Also, unity of beings is seen in the relationship of beings (persons) where the human encounters the Divine.

Again, another example of this is evident from Christian belief in the mystery of God that is seen as a Trinity of persons—the relationship of three persons (Father-Son-Spirit) in One God. Complementarity is the truth that relationship of two beings although distinct and polar opposites are unified in one life. Complementarity both in nature and among human beings is a manifestation that the mystery of the Divine is always seeking union with humanity. Whether we believe Divine to be Nature or a Divine Being, this is always the case.

The disruption of complementarity in nature and in humanity leads to a dislocation of relationships with others and a rupture within our own beings. This induces spiritual and mental pain. Each of us and certainly our society are divided and scattered at times. When we feel powerless over this and chose not to change our course of approaching reality differently and allow this malaise to sit with us, we are weak.

There are many parts of ourselves that we can no longer harmonize and feel drawn in different directions and are driven apart from each other and ultimately with ourselves. This takes many forms: by our desires and hopes that clash with our responsibilities at home; by our talents that seem wasted in our families or community and unrecognized for what they are; and by requests for help from others, all very legitimate, yet interfering without necessary private and time for reflection and prayer or interfering with our duties toward family. They take the shape of promises that stack up against us and pressure us beyond our limits of our time and energy.

This scattering is the anthesis of complementarity that holds relationships together. It takes the negative experiences of feeling tense and nervous—not at peace with those whom we love most and with whom we have cast our life to realize that something is desperately wrong. This causes serious disruptions where we have alienated friends, perhaps family, by our unfocused anger or rudeness, greed, or selfishness. It is disruptive when we have said and done things in spite of the situation that are foolish and imprudent, which others hold against us; we have overreacted to other's faults and refused forgiveness toward them. Whatever the circumstance and the reason, we are scattered and fractured. Because the effects show up within ourselves, the pain is severe. Working toward complementarity is not just allowing opposites to get along but allowing for the pain of separation to be treated by the healing pain of reconciliation. The pain of alienation becomes the means of reconciliation. This is true complementarity and healing that we need to strive for in relationships.

In summary, we have identified and processed how authentic relationship is essential to the human-Divine dynamic and allow us to speak of the divine mystery of faith in terms of five major attributes of human relationship: (1) dialogue of ongoing presence, (2) reciprocity, (3) interpersonal creativity generated by love, (4) the knowledge and love dyad, and (5) complementarity.

To put a human face on the Divine, I would like to relate it to an experience I had.

In 1981, as a young priest, I was approached by Tina, whose newborn son was diagnosed with spinal muscular atrophy (SMA) and prognosed to live a few weeks, so she requested baptism for her two-week-old son, Marc Anthony.

Recently I had the opportunity to catch up with Tina, to see how she was doing forty years later, and she was able to retell her story that changed her life and reinforced her faith in the Almighty.

You may ask how can this horrific ordeal transform into a blessing? That is the outcome when the presence of the Divine puts on a human face. In this case, the human face was a newborn.

Tina was so enthusiastic and joyful in expecting a third child that she began searching for a special outfit to bring the baby home. After a diligent search, she purchased a onesie with the image of a cloud and rainbow; unbeknownst to her at the time, this stretchy would become a significant symbol in this heartbreaking story. Within days of the infant's birth, it was evident that her son was in critical condition and was transported to the hospital. The infant struggled to move his head and couldn't cry, and according to Tina, his chest was "pushed in" due to muscular malfunction. The physician said Mark Anthony would not live more than three months at most.

I arrived at Columbia-Presbyterian Hospital to baptize Marc Anthony hoping his situation would improve. Tina desired a church christening for her family and her child—she wanted this to be special since Marc Anthony would not be with them for long. But since the child was baptized in the hospital, the Church would only celebrate the event by providing a postbaptismal ceremony. Tina was frustrated, angry, and confused that her son was not allowed by Church law to be baptized in a church with her family present. Later it was clarified to Tina that canon law of the Catholic Church recognizes the first baptism as the only baptism, and for pastoral reasons, the parish church could supply the ceremonies needed without a second baptismal ritual.

Disappointed but accepting this stipulation, Tina cherished each day with her son. She prayed each day with her faith in the Divine, strengthened that Marc Anthony was able to be present to her and vice versa for another day. Tina prayed for two things— that her son would not die alone and that he would pass while she held him. Although Tina remembers being overwhelmed with fear of dealing with the inevitable, she believed that her dying child radiated a love that kept her strong and her faith in God alive. She believed that if her child died in her arms, this would validate all the love she experienced by his short-lived life.

As days progressed, Marc Anthony's condition worsened and could only move his eyes toward the music from a music box adorned with butterflies.

Tina remarked to her husband that she hoped her son would pass wearing the onesie she bought for him before his birth. It seemed to be predestined, for shortly thereafter, one morning as Tina's two other children went downstairs to play, they asked if they could kiss their baby brother before going downstairs. The two children gave their baby brother a prolonged kiss before going to play, not knowing shortly after he would expire in Tina's arms.

Looking back retrospectively, the manner her two children kissed their brother was as if it was their final kiss saying goodbye. As Tina fondly remembers, Marc Anthony having trouble breathing took one last deep breath and expired. He died wearing the onesie Tina had treasured and in her arms, an answer to her prayers.

Although Tina experienced the unforgettable pain of losing a child, she remembers thanking God for the three months of radiant love received by Marc Anthony who gave her and her family indescribable joy and a presence of the divine in their lives. Tina sees the butterfly as a symbol of her son's presence within her heart. Now, every time she sees a butterfly, she feels Marc Anthony's presence.

This event resonates deep feelings within me as I heard it told by Tina forty years later. Thirty years prior to that situation in 1951, I was told by my mother years after my birth that I was diagnosed at six weeks old with a life-threatening congenital condition called pyloric stenosis, a condition where the muscular valve that connects the stomach to the top of the small intestines narrows and prevents food from passing out of the stomach. Ironically enough, I too was operated at the same hospital as Marc Anthony. Even strangely enough, I was baptized by a priest at the hospital since I was critically ill, and it was not known if I would survive the surgery, and two months later, I was brought to a postbaptismal ceremony.

Fortunately, I survived the ordeal and was able to author this book. The parallels here with Marc Anthony's condition are mind-boggling. Was this Divine intervention or not? All I know, seventy years later, I can tell this story and continue to have faith in the Divine and have God with me throughout my life. For me, throughout the years, both in ministry and as a clinician, I have experienced God with a human face in the lives of the people I was fortunate enough to serve.

Stories like these put a human face on the Divine. The miracle of life radiates love, the love that finds its origins in the Divine. For us to relate to the Divine, we need the inspiration and edification from events such as these where faith comes to life through the lives of people driving us to greener pastures whether in this life or hereafter.

I think when it comes to realizing what is faith in the Divine, we can take inspiration and reflect daily on the following prayer as found in the Jewish scriptures:

"You have been told O man and woman what is good and what the Lord requires of you: Only to do justice and to love kindness and walk humbly with your God" (Micah 6:8).

Chapter 5 Summary

- Relationship gives the Divine a human face.
- Relationship is key to perceive faith as human reality in search of divine mystery.
- To discuss the relationship of faith as it relates to the mystery of the divine, it is crucial that one understand the dynamics of human relationships.
- Relationship is the cornerstone of humanity seeking the Divine.
- Martin Buber emphasized the *I-Thou relationship* to what it means to be fully human.
- I-Thou relations are modeled on the Divine, where God is the Eternal, Thou.
- The primary characteristic of relationship is that it is an existential bond of sole presence between subjects for the sole purpose of each subject being for the other.
- Human relationship is ephemeral but has a spiritual dimension expressed in I-Thou relation.
- According to Buber, living in the world means that our being has two aspects: the aspect of experience perceived as I-It and the aspect of relationship perceived as I-Thou.
- The inborn Thou (natural self) realized in human relationship finds its consummation in the direct relationship to the Eternal Thou who is God.
- I-Thou relationship is a foretaste of the relationship of the human with the Divine.
- Characteristics of human relationship that mirror the Divine are—"dialogue of presence," exclusive reciprocity, unconditioned fidelity, interpersonal creativity resulting

from love, knowledge as fruit of the act of loving, and complementarity.

- The "dialogue of presence" exists as human soul to human soul and cannot be fully explained in language; it solely exists.
- Reciprocity as found in relationship is the result where two subjects share the mutual presence of being with each other.
- Fidelity as found in human friendship reflects the Jewish concept of *hesed*, that is, loving faithfulness.
- Interpersonal creativity is the actualization of love's power where self-transformation from self-interest to being self-gift to others happens.
- Knowledge and love collaborate in relationship leading to the discovery of one's true self and capacity to love another.
- Complementarity is rooted in nature contributing to the unity of the human race with nature.
- The Divine (God) is the origin of presence, reciprocity, interpersonal creativity, self-knowledge, love, and complementarity, which are all foundational aspects of human relationships.

Chapter 6

Ending with the Beginning

It gets late early.

—Yogi Berra

The end of human life springs life eternal. Endings come to pass with new beginnings. Time of this life passes without notice. Days, weeks, months, and years seem to pass through our fingers without pause. Before you come to full realization of your life, time is up! Age-wise, no one is promised tomorrow for time is the great equalizer.

There is a delightful Italian expression as one approaches the twilight of one's years—"*Prima di lasciare questo* mondo devo preparare il mio passaporto" translated to "Before I leave this world, I need to prepare my passport." This humorous saying emphasizes that I need to have all my accounts in order before the next destination. Even if one is fortunate to live a hundred years on this earth, life still is too short. With this in mind, we turn to the witty humor of the legendary baseball player Yogi Berra who is noted for his off the cuff remarks, later known as "Yogi-isms."[106] Yogi in describing playing left field at Yankee Stadium admitted it was tough to play during late autumn because the shadows would creep up on you and you had a tough time seeing the ball come off the bat—"*It gets late early out there.*"

We can take his remark and apply it to life. In baseball, when you are losing, the innings go by quickly. Halfway through the game, you realize you need to score runs, or you will lose for the game will soon be over. This is true in life. Living gets late early. We don't realize the passage of time until we approach our golden years. Then we reminisce about the old days and feel time is running out for us. As the Latin phrase goes, *tempus fugit*—"time flies"—whether you're having fun or not.

So too, in the world of faith, our convictions in life as noble as they may be, they are only temporary. What is not temporary is the destination that faith leads us to in the divine mystery. We will not be remembered for our personal accomplishments. What will be our legacy to our loved ones will be the generosity, faith, empathy, kindness, compassion, and love that we have exhibited. This and this only make a positive difference for our families, our friends, and all others we have had the opportunity to meet and work with in this life. These differences need not be marked with monuments and fanfare but be remembered eternally in the Book of Life.

The end is truly the beginning. We are born, we grow and develop, we learn, we work, we live with the joys and challenges of life, we love and then we die, but with death, we are not reborn but born into eternal life. In the words of Dr. Eben Alexander, recalling his odyssey experiencing the celestial realm of the Divine (cf. chapter 4), "We are born." Reborn suggested a time factor that our earthly existence gets recharged, revived, and resuscitated. This is not the case.

What faith in the divine mystery promises us is that we will be the same but yet radically different—we are *born into eternal life.* Remember that is how Francis of Assisi ends his universal prayer of love. We are the same because of "our likeness to the Divine"—our spirit continues, but we are totally different because we are no longer corporeal. The continuum of life we will experience thereafter is beyond linear time and space. In the hereafter, we will bring to consciousness what we have always been (there) and continue to be with no memory of a prior existence.

Once when I was facilitating a bereavement group of women who lost their partners, a frequently asked question was, is my husband or partner watching over me? One woman was particularly upset because she was worried if her deceased husband felt bad when she fell and broke her hip.

I remember my response to her is that I do not know, but those who pass on are in a different "stratosphere of existence" and her misfortune may not be of concern to him. As insensitive as this response may sound on the surface because I do not think any of us can adequately respond to her sentiment, I attempted to support her by redirecting her focus on a greater reality. What ultimately matters to a loved one left behind or moving on in the hereafter is the hope of reunification—forever. Hope is the great consolation faith promises.

I do not wish to speculate about the afterlife. What I can say is that faith gives us a radically different perspective of life. This perspective like many philosophies of life translates into the way people live their lives in the present. The existence of the Divine cannot be proven or disproven. Only through the faith we have embraced through our religious traditions, or through the transmission of family values held sacred throughout generations, or through personal human experience and observations of the wonders of our world, or through various cultural mores and myths, or finally with the spirituality that lies within us do we come to accept the Divine or not. One thing we learned from our reflections that we must always remember is that just because I cannot prove something empirically or historically doesn't imply that it is nonexistent.

Faith is the "ultra-proof" that I have termed, meaning that its reality is beyond and transcends the physical world of nature. Faith lives on by human testimony transmitted through generations attesting that the Divine can be experienced in life and affects the human condition of existence. The knowledge of faith is gratuitous, not earned or purchased. In Martin Buber's words, faith is the ultimate presence that involves the unity of being of two subjects succinctly manifested in the I-Thou relationship. For Jung, as we saw, faith is a calling for the self as "image of God" to be in dialogue with the ego (center of willing and striving of one's personality) so one comes to consciousness of one's wholeness. One's wholeness is full self-individuation that is the ultimate goal of being human. Jung believed the call to self-individuation attests to God's presence. We also saw how all this reverberates from Paul Tillich's thesis that all faith whether religious based or not is the foundation of what a person defines as their ultimate concern in life.

In this general sense, all humans experience faith. However, what kind and at what cost is another issue. The crux of the issue lies in whether nonreligious faith in humanity can evolve into faith in the Divine or not. This is where faith as gift is ultimately understood. The critical question arises then—if faith is a gift not earned or purchased for those who aspire to the Divine, what is the life course for human beings who lack this gift? What about those who lack this faith in the Divine? Deep down in my gut, this is a question for God to answer not for us to stand in judgment of the destiny of others.

Faith is very much alive and perennial in every period of history. Faith is both a concept and living entity that is difficult to grasp and too intricate to describe. Faith is not a phenomenon of nature but at the essence of humanity, visible in human behavior yet hidden in the recesses of the human heart. It is religious yet transcends religion. Faith is universal yet specifically concrete in human situations. Faith is infinitely variable yet remains constant. Faith is inherent in human nature, but it is always a gift that cannot be purchased or won, only accepted and cultivated. The indestructible essence of faith is that it is one's ultimate concern.

If faith is understood as what it centrally is, ultimate concern, it cannot be undercut by modern science, technology, or philosophy. And it cannot be discredited by its superstitions or authoritarian distortions within and outside churches, sects, and movements (not even social media).

Faith stands upon itself and justifies itself against those who attack it, because they can attack it only in the name of another faith. It is the triumph of the dynamics of faith that any denial of faith is itself an expression of faith, of an ultimate concern.[107]

Faith is not a theoretical affirmation of something uncertain. It is the existential acceptance of something or someone transcending ordinary experience. Faith is not an opinion but a state of being that redirects our perception of reality. Faith in a human being or in a

Divine being will affect the choices we make because of this change of perception.

We have explored how symbols are inherent in human endeavors. They are not merely signs. Symbols have a life of their own as living entities actualizing what they signify. We have already discussed how symbols are the language of faith as related to the light, the voice, and life of the Divine (cf. chapter 4), but another important symbol to consider when discussing faith in the Divine is the symbol of the circle.

The visual representation of the circle is the symbol *par excellence* describing infinity giving meaning to the expression—*ending with the beginning*. The symbol of the circle has been universally accepted by many philosophies, theologies, and in psychological circles, no pun intended, as meaning wholeness, original perfection, the Self, infinity, eternity, timelessness, communion, complete unity, and God.

Science too makes use of life symbols especially in the field of medicine. I remember as a youngster watching the TV medical series *Ben Casey* starring Vincent Edwards who played a young resident surgeon facing controversial subjects in a metropolitan hospital. The show was known for its opening titles, that consisted of a hand drawing the symbols—man (♂), woman (♀), birth (*), death (✝), and infinity (∞) accompanied by the voice of cast member Sam Jaffe intoning these symbols as they were drawn.

Geometrically, the circle is a derivative of the infinity symbol. Both symbols end with the beginning. The circle symbolizes the infinite movement of faith. The circle as symbol of the life of faith gives credence that life is an endless continuum of energy, light, and spiritual power. Death has no place in the circle of the life of faith since faith allows for the continuum of light, presence, and relationship and is not extinguishable. The circle exists with no beginning and no end. The circle is the perfect metaphor of faith ending with the beginning.

The life of faith in the human drama unfortunately becomes final with death. We have already stated that faith brings one to the "bridge of decision" whether to believe with a passage to eternal life—

to the world of the Divine. With death, faith ends, and depending upon one's conviction of religious belief, life continues in a celestial state of being where all reality is clearly experienced, and all is present in plain sight.

I often feel that we place an inordinate amount of emphasis on the feelings and thoughts of the grieving loved ones left behind, but what if those who have passed could possibly respond to these loved one as they move on to another reality? What does one say to loved ones who are left behind when someone dies? I like to quote from a beautiful love poem coming from the perspective of a speaker who is reflecting upon their own death. It is written not in fear of death but in order to comfort those who mourn. It was composed by David M. Romano in 1993 called "When Tomorrow Starts Without Me."

When tomorrow starts without me,
And I'm not there to see, If the sun should rise and find your eyes
All filled with tears for me;
I wish so much you wouldn't cry
The way you did today, While thinking of the many things,
We didn't get to say.
I know how much you love me,
As much as I love you,
And each time you think of me, I know you'll miss me too;
But when tomorrow starts without me, please try to understand,
That an angel came and called my name,
And took me by the hand,
And said my place was ready,
In heaven, far above
And that I'd have to leave behind
All those I dearly love.
But as I turned to walk away, A tear fell from my eye
For all my life, I'd always thought,
I didn't want to die.
I had so much to live for,
So much left yet to do, it seemed almost impossible,
That I was leaving you.

I thought of all the yesterdays,
The good ones and the bad,
The thought of all the love we shared,
And all the fun we had.
If I could relive yesterday,
Just even for a while,
I'd say good-bye and kiss you
And maybe see you smile.
But then I fully realized,
That this could never be,
For emptiness and memories,
Would take the place of me. And when I thought of worldly things
I might miss come tomorrow, I thought of you, and when I did
My heart was filled with sorrow. But when I walked through
            heaven's gates
I felt so much at home
When God looked down and smiled at me,
From His great golden throne,
He said, This is eternity,
And all I've promised you.
Today your life on earth is past
But here it starts anew.
I promise no tomorrow,
But today will always last, And since each day's the same way,
There's no longing for the past.
You have been so faithful,
So trusting and so true.
Though there were times
You did some things
You knew you shouldn't do.
But you have been forgiven and now at last you're free. So won't
     you come and take my hand and share my life with me?"
So when tomorrow starts without me,
Don't think we're far apart,
For every time you think of me,
I'm right here, in your heart.

What are the lessons learned from this excursion of faith? In summary, faith is the fundamental cornerstone of our being. Faith continues to inspire human wonder about the existence of the Divine beyond our deepest imagination. Faith invites us to come face to face to discover the core of our being and challenges us to be true to ourselves as responsible human beings. "The proof of faith" is not empirically based nor the result of a scientific formula or a law of nature but is exhibited in the human experience of living an unpredictable journey called life. "Believing in" can be a mental power of this journey where one has "razor-sharp" focus that seeks a life beyond this world. Truly human experiences in everyday living are experiences of faith and a possible gateway to the Divine. Faith as human reality opens one to the possibility of entering into divine mystery that is communion with the Divine.

I decided to go with the definition of faith as found in Hebrews 11:1 of the New Testament of the Bible: *"Faith is the assurance of things hoped for; the conviction of things not visibly seen."* I prefer this definition because faith is defined in terms of the results it obtains. Faith is an approach of possessing in advance what is hoped for, what we do not have now, a perception of accepting or knowing realities that are not visibly seen.

This twofold definition is not specifically religious. The first clause of this definition of knowing realities not seen is based upon a biblical mentality. Where the second clause of the definition, convictions about things unseen are intellectual based upon Greek philosophy. Convictions are conceptual not tangibly seen. It applies to relations between human persons. Here faith is of human reality. Social life is made up of human relations among people so faith is always present on the human level.

This definition of faith works by obtaining results whether it is accepting one's word when I cannot verify something but believing what one tells me is true or when a person promises to give me something that I trust, I possess already because of one's word. It is the *human act of faith* that is paramount. It is the relation between human persons that allows this faith act to be human reality. When faith in God is adherence to the person who is God, then I have faith as divine mystery.

The reality of the faith experience is enigmatic whether solely based upon trust in human relationships or faith in the divine mystery of God. For faith means many times I must lose to gain, die to live, be lost in order to be found, be in the last place to arrive at the first place. All these paradoxes are within the faith journey in life so that it is only when I am blind that I can really see, be deaf in order to hear, and lame in order to walk in the great reality of life we call faith.

Chapter 6 Summary

- Human life is precious but ephemeral; it is valued in terms of the enduring positive differences made to make the world a better place not solely by personal accomplishments.
- Linear time is finite, and fleeting for it passes without notice—"it gets late early."
- Faith teaches us endings are new beginnings.
- Faith in the Divine is the impetus for belief in one's final destination of eternal life.
- Faith in the Divine attests and promises of an afterlife where one is not reborn but born into eternal life with no recollection of a prior existence.
- Faith in the Divine can be associated with many factors such as religious traditions of many faiths, transmission of family values throughout generations, personal human experience and observation of wonders of our world that are unexplainable, cultural mores or myths, and the presence of spirituality of one's inner life.
- Faith in the Divine cannot prove God's existence any more than the physical sciences can prove or disprove this reality.
- The issue that arises that has no answer is that if faith in the Divine is exclusively gratuitous, what is the course of life for those who do not experience this gift?
- Faith is the "ultra-proof"—meaning it goes beyond the reality of empirical proof and beyond the physical laws of nature—it belongs to another "stratosphere of existence."
- As we observe nature, the universe, and the complexities of the human body, faith continues to incite human wonder about the existence of realities beyond us.

- Faith demands that we go beyond our deepest imagination to seek the core of our being.
- "The proof of faith" lies in being vulnerable to the human experience of living the unpredictable journey that life offers us.
- "Believing in" can be mental empowerment where one has "razor-sharp" focus in what is spiritually life giving.
- Truly human experiences in everyday ordinary lives are experiences of faith and can develop and transition as a possible gateway to the Divine.
- Faith is an inherent natural gift that opens up the possibility of encountering the Divine.
- The irony of faith is that it is universal yet specifically concrete. It allows for infinite variables yet constant.
- Faith whether present in a human person or in the existence of the Divine dictates our perception of reality and in turn directs our behaviors accordingly.
- The geometric symbol of the circle is a representation *par excellence* that defines the infinite scope of faith in the Divine—no beginning, no end—"ending with the beginning."
- The ultimate challenge of faith is that it challenges us to come face to face and discover the core of our being and be accountable as a responsible creature of this planet.
- Faith allows for the vulnerability that it is only when we are weak that we are strong, when we are blind that we can truly see; when we are deaf that we can truly hear, and when we are lame that we can walk in righteousness, justice, and truth.

Epilogue

In composing this work, it is my intent to provide a context in exploring faith as both human reality and divine mystery. My aim was not to establish a dichotomy or comparison between the two realities but demonstrate an interconnection and complementarity. It is my conviction that by understanding the familiar—faith in the human condition—it would incite us to appreciate the unfamiliar—faith in divine mystery. My purpose in so doing was to accentuate the complexity of the dynamic of faith and yet the simplicity of how it challenges our perception of reality. Faith is a natural gift shared by all human beings without prejudice. Faith has a multiplicity of meanings depending upon the context one uses the term. Like the reality of love, it has an unlimited range of possibilities and endless applications in life.

Authoring this book was providential in so far as in these challenging days, faith has been a frequent and comforting subject of conversation as we struggle with this global pandemic. I can't recall in my lifetime a word such as faith being so widely used among a diversity of people in dealing with the adversities we have experienced the past two years. Faith may not be the sole answer to our current dilemma, but it will undoubtedly lead us to a place of tranquility and resolve so that we can make levelheaded life decisions for ourselves and our families as we move forward.

My hope and prayer are that these reflections will lead us to understand and appreciate how in our lives we have come to faith, embrace it, and most of all share it with others.

As we have read in these pages, faith takes on many shapes and forms from personal commitment in human friendship to developing a spirituality that allows for a relationship with the Divine. It was my aim to present a fresh unique outlook highlighting faith in terms of the existential exigencies of life rather than solely define it in terms of religious or theological concepts. Faith truly becomes our ultimate concern in how we perceive reality.

Faith is an all-embracing permanent lifestyle not necessarily reflecting the fashion of the day but a constant reminder that we are accountable as human beings to be truthful, responsible, and at service of one another living on this planet. Whether one is a believer in the Divine or not, this accountability is a must. This accountability has to do with how we value human life and how responsible we are in treating others with respect and being true to ourselves. We have discussed how faith can be theological, and yet it can be religious. Faith can be philosophical, and it can be spiritual. Faith can be sociological and psychological. However, one thing it is above all—it is truly human. It is humanity that breathes life into faith. That breath originates with the Divine.

Faith is always identified with relationships. Without relationship, faith is not possible. Whether the relationship is between human beings or between the human with the Divine, faith is a surging, dynamic, and resilient movement from one being to another. Faith goes beyond individual disposition, political allegiance, or religious persuasion to make us conscious that there is a reality beyond us that we cannot master. Faith in the long run is a relentless journey we embrace to become more human. The journey to become unconditionally, fully, and totally human is the first step to becoming divine. The familiar saying, "To sin is human, but to forgive is to be divine," can be altered to say, "To be unconditionally, fully, and truly human is to be divine. Anything less needs forgiveness."

The pilgrimage of faith is likening to a nomad who is forever in search of a permanent home, a relentless search for life's meaning. One remains restless until faith is found and embraced. For the believer, the Divine can only be achieved if one remains true to the prime directive—to know and fully love the Other and to allow the Other to reciprocate this knowing and loving in return. This is the core of what it truly means to be human. Whether the Other is another human being or God, faith is our ultimate concern.

We have discovered a reoccurring representation of both the faith experience seen as a human reality and as a divine mystery in the symbol of **light**. In the vignettes presented in this book that are all true stories, the light of faith did inspire people and incite strength in them to conversion of heart to do great things. The en*light*enment born of faith results in human transformation where individuals put a human face on the Divine in their very lives. Ultimately, relationship is the key ingredient for faith to seek unity with the human and the Divine.

We have seen how the symbol of the circle accentuates the infinite pattern of life. The circle is an endless and ever living cycle of life in the universe. Faith sees the relationship of the Divine with humanity as symbolized by the circle having no beginning and no end.

As in the introduction, I described human destiny in terms of Dante's *Paradiso,* so too I conclude with this same classic to describe the Divine presence that awaits those who are faith-filled. In the following excerpt from the *Paradiso*, Canto I, Dante leaves purgatory where he has been purified of his sins and begins his journey with his beloved Beatrice to the Earthly Paradise atop Mount Purgatory. Beatrice is attracted to the sun, and the two begin to rise into the sky. Dante is awestruck, wondering whether he is having an out-of-body experience. As they ascend through the atmosphere, he and Beatrice pass through a layer of fiery light. Sensing Dante's curiosity about what is happening, Beatrice offers an explanation saying that all human souls have an *innate tendency* to rise toward God. It is God who draws Dante upward through the heavens. Here Dante begins his odyssey into the heavens, ten levels of heavens to be exact, and experiences the realm of the Divine encountering various personalities of human history on the way. Along with experiencing the celestial bodies of the universe, his soul ascends to the Source of Life.

Beatrice tells Dante that the *instinct implanted in the soul* is to rise, as fire rises toward the heaven; this belongs to the order of the universe, in which each part has its own function. Dante has been liberated from the distractions of his life on earth by the gift of his free will and now soars forward to communion with the Eternal Light.

> *The glory of Him who moveth everything*
> *Doth penetrates the universe, and shine In one part more and*
> *in another less. Within that heaven which most his*
> *light receives Was I, and things beheld which to repeat*
> *Nor knows, nor can, who from above demands; Because in*
> *drawing near to its desire*
> *Our intellect ingulphs itself so far,*
> *Truly whatever of the holy realm*
> *I had the power to treasure in my mind*
> *Shall now become the subject of my song...*
> *O power divine, lend'st thou thyself to me So that the shadow of the*
> *blessed realm Stamped in my brain I can make manifest*
> *Thou'll see me come unto thy darling tree, And crown myself*
> *thereafter with those leaves which the theme and thou*
> *shall make me worthy...*
> (Translation—courtesy of The Literature Network website)

That *innate tendency* and that *instinct implanted* in the soul to rise toward God as mentioned in canto I is faith. That attraction and movement of Dante's ascent to God is the work of faith. Dante is no longer distracted from the lures of this world but seeks the Eternal light that leads to endless life.

The canto continues:

> *O Love whose rule the heavens attest,*
> *Thou know'st, who with thy light didst lift my state.*
> *When that the wheel that thou eternizest In longing, held me*
> *with the harmony*
> *Which, thou attunes and distinguishes,*
> *So much of heaven was fired, it seemed to me, With the sun's*
> *blaze that never river or rain*
> *Widened the waters to so great a sea.*
> *The new sound and the great light made me fain*

With craving keener than he had ever been
Before in me, their cause to ascertain. She (Beatrice) then,
who saw me as I myself within,
My mind's disturbance eager to remit, Opened her lips before I
could begin, And spoke: "Thou makest thyself dense of wit
With false fancy, so that thou dost not see What thou would'st
see, wert thou but rid of it.
Thou'rt not on earth as thou supposes thee:
But lightning from its own place rushing out
Ne'er sped as thou, who to thy home dost flee."
(Translation by Laurence Binyon in the edition of Dante's
Paradiso, London: MacMillan and Co. Ltd. 1952)

Dante is awestruck by Beatrice's remark—what if those imped-iments that distract one from the Divine presence as they were in Dante's odyssey be removed in earthly life? Would more on the earth succumb to the mystery of faith in the Divine?

Dante's vision of the heavens

Notes

[1] Wystan Hugh Auden (1907–1973) was an Anglo-American poet noted for his stylistic and technical finesse in works of politics, morals, love, and religion.

[2] Albert Einstein (1879–1955) was a German born theoretical physicist who developed the theory of relativity, one of two pillars of modern physics.

[3] Clive Staples Lewis (1898–1963) was a prolific Irish writer and scholar who held academic positions in English literature at Oxford and Cambridge Universities. He was best known for his works of fiction, especially *The Screwtape Letters, The Chronicles of Narnia, and The Space Trilogy.*

[4] Ibid.

[5] The Bible. RSV edition (San Francisco: Ignatius Press, 2006).

[6] English Oxford Living Dictionary (London: Oxford University Press, 2019). Definition of faith.

[7] Ibid.

[8] St. Thomas Aquinas was one of the greatest of scholastic philosophers of the thirteenth century who produced a comprehensive synthesis of Christian theology and Aristotelian philosophy that influenced Roman Catholic doctrine for centuries.

[9] Ibid.

[10] Ibid.

[11] St. Anselm of Canterbury (1033–1109) defended Church's interests in England. He was known as "father of scholasticism" established a medieval school of philosophy that made use of the critical method of philosophical analysis that dominated teaching in the medieval universities in Europe from about 1100–1700 AD. He held that faith necessarily precedes human reason but human reason can expand faith (Latin: *fides quarens intellectum*). He was quoted as saying, "…I do not seek to understand that I may believe but believe that I might understand."

[12] Rene Descartes ((1596–1650) was a French-born philosopher, mathematician, and scientist. Descartes is widely regarded as one of the founders of modern philosophy during the age of enlightenment in seventeenth-century Europe. He was a great proponent of rationalism that challenged much of medieval scholastic thinking of Western philosophy. The major theme of his philosophy was "I think therefore I am."

13 Soren Kierkegaard (1813–1855) was a Danish philosopher, theologian, poet, social critic, and religious author who is widely considered to be the first existential philosopher. Much of his philosophy deals with the issues of how one lives as a "single individual" giving priority to concrete human reality over abstract thinking and highlighting the importance of personal choice and commitment.

14 Michael Watts, *Kierkegaard* (London: One World Publishers, 2003), 4–6. Also cf. Walter Lowrie, *Kierkegaard's Attack upon Christendom* (New Jersey: Princeton Press, 1969), 37–40.

15 Paul Tillich, *Dynamics of Faith* (New York: Harper One Publishers, 1957), 1–4.

16 Ibid., 4f.

17 Ibid.

18 Ibid., 7.

19 Ibid., 10f.

20 St Augustine of Hippo, *Confessions of St. Augustine*. Autobiographical work of Augustine of Hippo consisting of thirteen books written in Latin between 397 and 400 AD. The work outlines his sinful youth and the process of his conversion to Christianity.

21 *Dynamics of Faith*, op. cit., 52.

22 Rudolf Otto, *The Idea of the Holy* (London: Oxford University Press, 1958).

23 *Dynamics of Faith*. op. cit., 15.

24 Ibid., 33.

25 James W. Fowler, *Stages of Faith: The Psychology of Human Development and Quest for Meaning* (New York: Harper One, 1979).

26 Daniel J. Levinson, *The Seasons of a Man's Life* (New York: 1978).

27 *Stages of Faith: The Psychology of Human Development*, op. cit.

28 Wallace B. Clift, *Jung and Christianity: The Challenge of Reconciliation* (New York: Crossroads, 2000).

29 Pope Francis's pastoral visit to Iraq March 5–8. Pope Francis met with Ayatollah Ali al-Sistani in Najaf, Iraq.

30 Nihilism is a philosophy or family of views within philosophy expressing some form of negation toward life or toward fundamental concepts such as knowledge, existence, and the meaning of life. Some nihilist positions hold that human values are baseless, that life is meaningless, and that knowledge is impossible.

31 Friedrich Nietzsche, *Beyond Good and Evil* (New York: Vintage Books, 1966).

32 Ibid.

33 Friedrich Nietzsche, *Thus Spoke Zarathustra* (1883).

34 Ibid.

35 Sir Alfred Hitchcock (1899–1980) was an English film director, producer, and screenwriter. He was known as "master of suspense." He directed over fifty featured films in a career spanning six decades becoming one of the most influential and widely studied filmmakers in the history of cinema.

36　Pope John Paul II was the head of the Catholic Church and sovereign of the Vatican City State from 1978 to 2005.

37　Edgar Allan Poe (1809–1849) was an American writer, poet, editor, and literary critic. He was best known for his poetry and short stories, particularly his tales of mystery and the macabre. He is widely regarded as the central figure of romanticism in American literature as a whole, and he was one of the country's earliest practitioners of the short story.

38　Former President Barak Obama challenged youth activists on their "purity" and "judgmentalism" objecting to the prevalence of "call out culture" and "wokeness" during an interview at the Obama Foundation Summit held on October 29, 2019, discussing leadership, grass roots change, and the power places have to shape our journeys. This was reported in the New York Times article: *Obama on Call-Out Culture: "That's Not Activism"* by Emily S. Rueb and Derrick Bryson Taylor published on October 31, 2019, and updated on August 10, 2020.

39　Rollo May, *Man's Search for Himself* (New York: Dell Publishing, 1953), 14f.

40　T. S. Eliot, "The Hollow Men," in Collected Poems (New York: Harcourt, Brace, and Co., 1934), 101.

41　Man's Search for Himself, op. cit., 37.

42　Neurosis or neurotic anxiety was the former terminology used in psychiatry to define anxiety symptoms that cause clinically significant distress or impairment in social, occupational. or other important areas of functioning as indicated currently in *The Diagnostic and Statistical Manual of Mental Disorders DSM-5* (2013). The diagnoses of neurotic anxiety or neurosis had been replaced with a new classification of anxiety disorders that include disorders that share features of excessive fear and anxiety and related behavioral disturbances. Neurosis or neurotic anxiety was the psychiatric classification identified by Sigmund Freud (1856–1939) to describe a psychological condition that was treated by psychoanalysis to uncover unconscious unresolved conflict responsible causing this medical condition

43　*Man's Search for Himself.* op. cit., 45.

44　Ibid., 46f.

45　Ibid., 48.

46　Ibid.

47　Baruch Spinoza was a Dutch philosopher and one of the early thinkers of the Age of Enlightenment in seventeenth-century Europe and also a modern biblical critic. He believed that God is the sum of the natural and physical laws of the universe and endorsed pantheism.

48　*Man's Search for Himself*, op. cit., 55f.

49　Ibid., 61.

50　Ibid., 63.

51　Ibid.

52　Ibid., 64.

53 Ibid.
54 Ibid., 68.
55 Ibid., 68–69.
56 Ibid., 72.
57 William Wordsworth (1770–1850) was an English Romantic poet who with Samuel Taylor Coleridge launched the Romantic Age in English Literature; author of 523 sonnets (popular form of poetry during the Romantic period).
58 *Man's Search for Himself.* op. cit., 75.
59 *Dynamics of Faith.* op. cit., 47.
60 *Jung and Christianity.* op. cit., 51.
61 *Dynamics of Faith.* op., cit. 49.
62 *Jung and Christianity.* op. cit., 53.
63 *Dynamics of Faith.* op. cit., 49.
64 Ibid., 50.
65 Definition of religion in the Merriam Webster Dictionary.
66 *Dynamics of Faith.* op. cit., 52.
67 Ibid.
68 Ibid., 53.
69 Ibid., 54.
70 Ibid., 55.
71 Francis I. Andersen, "On Reading Genesis 1–3," in *Backgrounds for the Bible.* Edited by Michael Patrick O'Connor and David Noel Freedman (Pennsylvania: Penn State University Press, 1987).
72 *Jung and Christianity.* op. cit., p.60.
73 *Dynamics of Faith.* op. cit., p.58.
74 Carl G. Jung was a Swiss psychiatrist and psychoanalyst, founded analytical psychology. He is noted for his concept of individuation—lifelong psychological process of differentiation of the self. He formulated twelve universal mythic characters residing within our unconscious. They include the ruler, creator/artist, sage, the innocent, the explorer, the rebel, the hero, the wizard, the jester, "every man or every woman," lover, and caregiver. These symbolic images unconsciously understood and defined the range of basic human motivations. Jung in extrapolating his theory of the psyche identified four major archetypes: the *self* (sense of unity in experience with the goal of self-actualization), the persona or mask (which is the outward face we present as the desirable self to the world), the *shadow*, (the animal side of personality, which is irrational, instinctive, and impulsive), and *the anima, animus* (the true self and primary source of communication with collective unconscious).
75 Carl Jung. *Collected Works*, IX(I), 154.
76 Tillich understands that a myth that is understood as myth, but not removed or replaced as a "broken myth." Christianity denies by its very nature any broken myth because of its presupposition of the first commandment: the affirmation of the ultimate (God) as ultimate (God) and the rejection of any kind of idolatry.

[77] *Dynamics of Faith*. op. cit., 61f.

[78] Christianity adherents worldwide 2.382 billion (31.11%) of estimated world's population of 7,830,458,560 as of March 2020 according to United Nations Population Division.

[79] Ibid. Judaism adherents worldwide 14.7 million 0.18% of global population.

[80] Ibid. Islam adherents worldwide 1.193 billion 24.9% of global population.

[81] José Enrique Aguilar Chiu et al., eds, *The Paulist Biblical Commentary*. Albert Vanhoye, S. J., *Commentary on Hebrew* (Mahwah, New Jersey: Paulist Press, 2018) 1510.

[82] Keith E. Swartley, *Encountering the World of Islam* (Westmont.: Inter Varsity Press, 2005).

[83] Quran 95:6.

[84] Teresa of Calcutta (Mother Mary Teresa Bojaxhiu) was an Albanian-Indian Roman Catholic nun and missionary who founded the missionaries of charity dedicated to serve the poor, managing homes for people dying of HIV/AIDS, leprosy, and tuberculosis.

[85] *Jung and Christianity*. op. cit., 105.

[86] Ibid. 104.

[87] Carl Jung, *Memories, Dream, Reflections* (1961). Jung directed that this autobiography not be included in the collected works of his writings and not be published until after his death fearing the possible criticism it would receive since this work was too personal and too uncommon at the time.

[88] C. G. Jung, *Collected Works*, XII. ed. Sir Herbert Read et al. trans. RFC Hull, 2nd edition rev.; Bollinger Series (Princeton, New Jersey: Princeton University Press, 1970), 87.

[89] *Jung and Christianity*. op. cit., 110.

[90] *Collected Works*, XI. op. cit., 87.

[91] Areopagus is a prominent rock located northwest of the Acropolis in Athens, Greece. In classical times, it was the location of a court that tried cases of deliberate homicide, religious matters, as well as cases involving arson of olive trees. In classical Greek mythology, Ares was supposedly tried by the gods on the Areopagus for the murder of Poseidon's son Halirrhothius. The Areopagus, like most city-state institutions, continued to function in Roman times, and it was from this location, drawing from the potential significance of the Athenian altar to the *Unknown God* that the Apostle Paul is said to have delivered a famous speech (Acts17:24–18:1).

[92] Athanasius of Alexandria (c. 296–373 CE) was a Christian theologian of the patristic period (late first century to end of eight century CE) who was a staunch defender of the Christian doctrine of the Incarnation of Jesus Christ and the Trinity. The quotation "God became man so that man might become God" is attributed to him in defining the doctrine of the Incarnation of Christ.

[93] E. Alexander MD, *Proof of Heaven-A Neurosurgeon's Journey into the Afterlife* (New York: Simon and Schuster, 2012), 29–33.

[94] Ibid. p. 38–39.

[95] Ibid. p. 48–49.

[96] Marcus Tullius Cicero (106 BCE–43 BCE) was a Roman statesman, lawyer scholar, philosopher, and notably one of Rome's greatest orators and prose stylists.

[97] Francis of Assisi c.1181/1182–1226 CE. Giovanni, renamed Francesco, in full Francesco di Pietro di Bernardone venerated as St. Francis of Assisi, was an Italian Catholic friar, deacon, mystic, preacher, and founder of the men's order of Friars minor. Francis is universally acclaimed as saint of ecology and of animals for his esteemed reverence for the natural environment as the work of God's creation and his patronage of animals as creatures of God.

[98] Martin Buber (1878–1965) was an Austrian Jewish philosopher known for his philosophy of dialogue, a form of existentialism centered on the distinction between the I-Thou relationship and the I-It relationship. In 1923, he wrote his famous essay on existence *Ich und Du* (German) later translated into English in 1937 as *I and Thou*.

[99] Martin Buber, *I and Thou*. Part I, trans. Walter Kaufmann (New York: Simon & Schuster, Touchstone edition, 1970), 55–56.

[100] Ibid. p. 59f.

[101] Maurice S. Friedman, *Martin Buber: The Life of Dialogue* (New York: Routledge, 2002), 4th ed. Chapter 12: The Eternal Thou.

[102] Erich Fromm (1900–1980) was a German social psychologist, psychoanalyst, sociologist, humanistic philosopher, and democratic socialist noted for his writings on humanism, social theory, Marxism, being and having as modes of existence, security versus freedom, social character, and character orientation.

[103] Ludwig Philipp Albert Schweitzer, OM, was an Alsatian-German religious philosopher, musicologist, and medical missionary in Africa especially known for founding the Schweitzer Hospital providing unprecedented medical care for the natives of Lambarene, Gabon.

[104] Erich Fromm, *The Art of Loving* (New York: Harper and Row Publishers, 1956), 28–29.

[105] R. A. Nicholson, *Rumi* (London: George Allen and Unwin Ltd., 1950), 122–23. Jalal ad Din Mohammad Rumi was a thirteenth-century Persian poet, Islamic scholar, Maturdi theologian, and Sifi mystic.

[106] Lawrence Peter "Yogi" Berra (1925–2015) was an outstanding baseball player and Hall of Famer who played nineteen seasons (1946–1963, 1965) for the New York Yankees. He was an American professional baseball catcher who was an eighteen-time All Star and won ten World Series.

[107] *Dynamics of Faith*. op. cit., 147.

About the Author

Louis Marini, MS, MSW, MDiv, JCL, through his multidisciplinary expertise and experience in pastoral ministry as a former Catholic priest of seventeen years, an ecclesiastical jurist, a researcher, an educator, and a clinician in the areas of psychology, social work, theology, and canon law, shares his reflections concerning the relevance of faith in our time. He hopes to offer solace to former patients, students, and parishioners to whom he had served in the past along with you the reader. He received his graduate degrees from the Catholic University of America, Washington, DC; Fordham University, New York City; Iona College, New Rochelle, New York; and St. Joseph Seminary, Yonkers, New York. He completed postgraduate work at the Minuchin Center for the Family New York City (1999) and studies in chemical dependency at Maxwell Institute in Tuckahoe, New York (2000–2001). He was a member of the American Psychological Association and the National Association of Social Workers until 2020 upon retirement after twenty-four years of clinical practice as a counseling psychologist and family psychotherapist.

CPSIA information can be obtained
at www.ICGtesting.com
Printed in the USA
BVHW031550100422
633502BV00001B/5

9 781662 472558